LIFE INTO ART

LIFE INTO ART
Italo Svevo and the Novel

PETER DAVIES

Greenwich Exchange
London

Greenwich Exchange, London

First published in Great Britain in 2021
All rights reserved

Printed and bound by imprintdigital.com
Cover design by December Publications
Tel: 07951511275

Greenwich Exchange Website: www.greenex.co.uk

Cataloguing in Publication Data is available
from the British Library

ISBN: 978-1-910996-50-8

for Libby

CONTENTS

1

Introducing Italo Svevo

NEARLY A CENTURY AFTER THE PUBLICATION of his masterpiece *La coscienza di Zeno* in 1923, it is no exaggeration to say that the name of Italo Svevo still needs an apologia. In conversation with well-read individuals who will immediately be able to place and have something to say about the works of Proust, Kafka, James Joyce, Robert Musil, Thomas Mann, and Henry James, as pioneer representatives of the modern European novel, it is still possible to have to add riders when introducing the figure of Svevo into the discussion.

There are a number of reasons for this, none of them necessarily familiar to the common phenomenon of neglected genius. From the outset Svevo was ignored in his own country. But even that is not quite true. For what is Svevo's 'own country'? Italy now gratefully claims him. But although he wrote in (a self-invented species of) Italian, the Trieste into which he was born, as Aron Ettore Schmitz, and passed most of his life was a city of the Austro-Hungarian Empire, its greatest port and outlet on the world of maritime trade. Svevo was an Austrian citizen until his late fifties, when Trieste became an Italian city on the dismemberment of Austria-Hungary in the wake of the First World War. His working life, in first banking and later industry and commerce, looked towards Vienna, even London, rather than Rome.

His upbringing had been in Germany and his education was in German, in which he was fluent and in whose literature he was well read. He also spoke excellent French, the language in which his wife Livia often addressed him, especially in her letters. Later, as head of operations in London of the Veneziani underwater anti-fouling paint company he acquired a certain amount of English.

The nearest he came to speaking Italian was the rugged Triestine dialect, which was his everyday language. This is still spoken in Trieste, but as used in the 19th century it had a greater Slovene, Croatian, Serbian, and even some Greek, linguistic component than it does today.

So it was perhaps not surprising that when in the 1890s Svevo's first two, self-published, novels, *Una vita* (1893) and *Senilità* (1898) were subjected to the scrutiny of Italian critics they were not liked. Italy was at that time a country without a true novel-writing tradition. Its novels were singular – sometimes admittedly striking – excrescences in a literary landscape whose most celebrated prominences were the works of its poets. There was no sense of a steady development of the form as was discernible in the novel-writing traditions of England, France and, by then catching up, Germany. By the time Svevo began to write, the novel in these countries was moving away from Romanticism, through realism and naturalism (not to be confused) to the beginnings of modernism.

The revered, romantic (and frequently unreadable) *I promessi sposi* of Manzoni, though written in 1827, still stood at that time as an apparently unsurpassable peak of Italian novelistic culture. Verdi had begun his famous *Requiem* to celebrate a fellow composer, Rossini, but it ended up as a homage to Manzoni.

Language itself was an important consideration for Italian writers of the era. They worshipped style and cultivated a careful choice of words and phrases. In this search they looked to the purest and most elegant Tuscan for their model. Svevo turned his back on the pursuit of this kind of purity. He could not abide Manzoni – a heresy in those times. Nor did he try to graft his native dialect on to standard Italian as the Sicilian Giovanni Verga had successfully done. Svevo attempted something completely different, but something not as readily to be understood. He chose to create his own version of Italian from the blunt, pared-down utterances of the financial and commercial community he knew so well – its clerks as well as its bosses.

This doesn't produce a particularly aesthetic result. It brings into the Italian novel nothing to match the mystery and remoteness of Verga's *Sicilia sconosciuta*. It's been often said – by Italians – that Svevo's version of their language reads like a bad translation from a foreign tongue.

The Italian critics who first read his novels recoiled from this ugliness – its sheer strangeness. How on earth, for example, could any novelist have his characters speaking to each other in the remote-sounding past historic tense rather than the present perfect of normal conversational usage? Svevo's bank clerks were made to sound like men clumsily aping primitive mediaeval chroniclers as they traded their threadbare mundanities at their desks.

Objections to Svevo were even more violent against his matter than his style. The Italian romantic hero, as created by the overcharged prose of Gabriele D'Annunzio, was de rigueur in the novel of the 1880s and 1890s, in a nation gradually finding its feet and self-esteem, as it acquired more territory and sought greater recognition among the major European powers. Italian readers and critics were simply not ready to understand the neurasthenic 'modern' world of the *inetti*, the inept, failed men, floundering in their third-rate aspirations, who peopled Svevo's pages, seemingly without any power to help – or even to want to help – themselves to betterment.

Even James Joyce, that indefatigable proselytizer for writers whom he felt undervalued (whose ranks naturally included himself!), declared in puzzlement that he could do nothing to part the curtain of silence that fell over Svevo's work in his native city. He was quietly informed by the president of Trieste's cultural academy, the Società di Minerva, that Svevo's writings were too negative and 'unpatriotic' to sit well with the nationalistic aspirations of Italian Triestines.

So when Svevo did have his moment of breakthrough, with the publication of *La coscienza di Zeno*, after the First World War we are not to imagine this as a moment of national éclat, with Italy, now among the victors of the war, proudly acclaiming a new literary son. His recognition had been almost entirely due to the anglophone Irishman James Joyce who had earlier perceived his genius after reading *Senilità*, and lobbied for him in Paris literary circles. Svevo's gradual recognition as the father of the modern Italian novel was very much a private affair among a like-minded coterie, largely non-Italian: Joyce; Valery Larbaud; the translators Benjamin Crémieux and his wife Marie-Anne Comnène; and Ilya Ehrenburg, an early Soviet admirer. Eugenio Montale became an early Italian fan, as was Umberto Saba, Trieste's celebrated poet.

Non-literary, mercantile Trieste remained indifferent. *La coscienza di Zeno*, which had, like its predecessors, been published at its author's own expense, was also given the cold shoulder in wider Italy.

At this moment the march of non-literary history was not on Svevo's side, as he and other Triestines were to find out after the heady first moments of November 1918. In the immediate postwar period liberal political impulses had been towards the preservation of the city's socialist tradition; co-operation with the Slovene population (at that time larger than that of Slovenia's own capital Ljubljana); and special protection for Triestine shipping, Istrian agriculture and local industry.

But these tendencies soon sank under an aggressive ultra-conservative nationalism. Throughout Italy new, dark forces were on the move. Trieste's irredentists, (Svevo amongst them) who had welcomed the landing of Italian troops on this Austrian territory on 3 November 1918, soon found themselves elbowed aside by fascist leaders from Milan, whose thuggish methods found it easy to foment mob unrest in this hitherto tolerant, multiracial city. One of its early victims was the Narodni Dom, Trieste's Slovene cultural centre, which housed a library, bank, church and educational facilities; all these buildings were burnt down by the mob in June 1920.

Triestine acceptance of such violence in the service of its new-found nationalism became sadly indistinguishable from the fascism to which Italy was becoming increasingly in thrall. Triestines were to find that they had, in effect, exchanged rule from Vienna to rule from a Rome which found no reason to distinguish either it or other postwar frontier territorial gains from Austria, such as Trentino, Udine or Fiume, all proud of their own linguistic cultures, by special treatment.

Italy had plenty of ports of its own and did not need another in the far northeast. Trieste swiftly declined from its international status as the Austrian Adriatic entrepôt to a provincial Italian city, a port without a hinterland, cut off now from direct access to Vienna by the newly founded Kingdom of Yugoslavia immediately to the north.

Mussolini's 1922 March on Rome and his subsequent consolidation of fascist power throughout the institutions of the Italian state marked the end of democracy in Italy, not to be restored until 1945. It also guaranteed that whatever plaudits Svevo might garner elsewhere in the world (and they were slow enough in coming) it would not be until long after his death in 1928 following a car crash, long after the Second World War in fact, that he began to be properly recognized in Italy.

Where Italy simply ignored him, literary opinion in England, at that time, led by the *Times Literary Supplement*, was at first to deride him in contemptuous terms. When in January 1926 Montale attempted an apologia, in the periodical *Il Quindicinale*, of Svevo's typical 'European man', not as a heroic figure of 'cosmopolitan visions' but as one of the 'heirs of thousand-year-old ills and grandeurs, exiles and outcasts of a civilization that is swallowing itself up', *TLS* rebuked him with John Bullish robustness. 'This defence is not one that need necessarily be accepted; indeed in our view, it needs to be combated. It will certainly be combated in Italy, whose new and forcible political faith, yet to become a genuine inspiration in literature, will certainly not find that positive element on which it prides itself, in the grotesque domestic vicissitudes of the gelatinous "European" Zeno Cosini, the autobiographical hero of this book.'

Such a ringing endorsement of fascist dictatorship as a tool with which to attack an innovative literary artist such as Svevo beggars belief. Chillingly, for our own times, the derision aimed by this *TLS* (anonymous) critic at what he described as Svevo's 'gelatinous "European"' might easily have dropped from the lips of current-day English Europhobe demagogues.

Significantly, when a bust of Svevo, commissioned and executed at the family's expense, was unveiled in Trieste's Giardino pubblico in 1931, the only speeches permitted on the occasion by the authorities were those which dwelt on his prominence as a 'patriot'. (Svevo had, to his great amusement, received a civic honour for his contribution to Italian trade!) Larbaud and Crémieux were ignored, and a deeply felt telegram from Joyce was, conspicuously not read out as part of the ceremony. In 1942 the bust was torn down by the Fascists.

Fascism was not to touch Svevo and his family in his lifetime on the score of their Jewish ancestry. Until the advent of Nazism, Mussolini's Italy would not go so far. It was only during the Second World War that these antecedents became an issue. In 1943 his widow Livia, unable to contemplate raising the huge bribe required by the authorities, to become registered as an Aryan, revealed, in a moment of extreme agitation, that she was a quarter Jewish. In immediate peril as a result of this admission, she was compelled to flee Trieste for her life and spent the remainder of the war in hiding in a small town near Treviso, in the hills above the River Piave. There she worked intermittently on her memoir of her late husband, *Vita di mio marito* (published, 1950; revised, 1958).

The effect of these colliding events and prejudices – Svevo's coming on the scene just as an Italy of which he was newly a citizen was falling prey to malignant dreams of Imperial Rome – was to stunt Svevo's appreciation in Italy for decades. As late as the mid-1960s it was still possible to drop his name, or that of his masterpiece, into discussion among an otherwise literate, well-read class of Italian students on a university summer school, only to be greeted by mystified incomprehension.

In literary cultures and countries other than his own he fared better. France was to know him early on, thanks to the exertions of Larbaud and Crémieux. In the English-speaking world, *TLS*'s philistine verdict was, luckily, not to be the last word. Publication of *La coscienza di Zeno* in English by Knopf in America as *Confessions of Zeno* in a quite brilliant translation by Beryl de Zoete in 1930, suddenly brought this new author to notice in the anglophone world.

Reviewing it in the London periodical *Bookman* later that year Vita Sackville-West pronounced it 'a book for all the world, one which must be placed on the shelf just below *Don Quixote*, and certainly in the company of the finest novels of our own day.' An equally felicitous translation of *Senilità* by de Zoete followed hot on its heels, entitled *As a Man Grows Older* (Joyce's choice of title), in 1932. *Una vita* had to wait another thirty years until its translation into English by Archibald Colquhoun as *A Life* in 1963.

If, in the intervening years the name of Svevo had seemingly rather gone 'off the boil' even in the English-speaking world, it was to be revived by Secker and Warburg, who had from the early 1960s begun to assemble its five-volume Uniform Edition of extant translations of Svevo's work, based around his three major prose works. In the Sixties, too, a new young generation of English enthusiasts, stifled by the increasing parochiality of the English (though not the American) postwar novel, and avid for all kinds of modern European writing, was also discovering Svevo, thanks to the affordable Penguin paperback editions of de Zoete's translations.

The year 1966 saw the first substantial critical biography in any language, P.N. Furbank's excellent *Italo Svevo: The Man and the Writer*. It has, I think, not really been surpassed for its insight and understanding of its complex subject. This was succeeded in English by Brian Moloney's *Italo Svevo* (1974) in the Writers of Italy series, and John Gatt-Rutter's *Italo Svevo: A Double Life* (1988), probably the most comprehensive account to date.

In the face of this activity the Italian publishing industry has been busy over the last few decades, with new editions of all aspects of Svevo's output, including a number of his many plays. This process has been accompanied by a flow of secondary literature in Italian. A good deal of it is biographical in nature, or deals with matters of style, influences, etc, rather than tackling the novels and their author's stature in world literature head on.

Perhaps this is to be expected. There is still a sense of faint uneasiness in Italy about the nature of Svevo's acceptance. There is always a lingering feeling that the 'case' of Svevo needs a specific defence. He may be seen as a Triestine regionalist; or his Jewish antecedents (almost entirely invisible as preoccupations in the novels) are adduced as a reason for his hero's outlook. Zeno has variously been seen as the literary incarnation of what became especially familiar in American-Yiddish culture, the *schlemiel*, that constitutionally hopeless individual who had in fact sprung to birth in the novella *Peter Schlemihls wundersame Geschichte* by the French-born German author Adelbert von Chamisso as early as 1814. And there has always hung over Italian critics the unspoken consciousness of having had Svevo discovered for them by foreigners, of having failed somehow to rise themselves to the level of events, at a period when the recognition of his genius was offered to them. At the same time Svevo's failure to exhibit a recognizably Italian style of genius is sometimes held against him. His mentality is so manifestly closer to that of, say, the Austrian Robert Musil, than it is to any other Italian author.

As for Trieste, these days it has come wholeheartedly to embrace its prodigal son. Among the tourist literature of hotels and restaurants it greets you with at its railway station is a street plan, 'The Trieste of Italo Svevo'. It is these days a charming city, but it feels 'cut-off' from the rest of Italy as you approach from Venice by rail, along its narrow coastal strip with the steep slopes leading up behind the town to the stony plains of the limestone Carso at its back, and the frontier of Slovenia only a few kilometres away.

There are still more than mere vestiges of the feel of the Austrian fin de siècle about some of its hotels, still with their spacious, elegant correspondence rooms now no longer used for that purpose by the Austrian and Triestine businessmen for whom they were designed. Its port is these days a recipient, rather, of tourist cruises than a centre of the hectic mercantile atmosphere that was once its lifeblood.

The city fathers have since changed their minds about their famously eccentric genius. A small Svevo Museum, founded in 1997, carries the flame for him and his works, linking him at the same time with his mentor James Joyce in a twin institution housed in the same building on the city's Via della Donna del Mare.

2

Neglect – and discovery

BY 1919, WHEN SVEVO WAS READY to embark on writing *La coscienza di Zeno*, he had lived most of his life. He was the author of two published novels. These had admittedly been largely neglected, but certainly not completely ignored. Even the severest criticism (and there had been no shortage of that) is, after all, a form of recognition. Nevertheless their neglect had been instrumental in determining him to turn his back on his literary aspirations.

He had also been a literary journalist on the small stage of Triestine cultural life, and had written a number of plays, none of which had been published or performed. Yet he continued to the end of his life to think of himself as a man of the theatre and one of his very last works was a play, *La rigenerazione* (*Regeneration*) – virtually the only one to be translated into English.

But, as it has frequently been pointed out, his true genius as a writer did not lie in making the characters that germinated in his brain come alive in spoken dialogue. The drama of the rumination inside the brain of Zeno, who never tires us with the conversation he holds with himself, does not work effectively when it is called on to be uttered on stage. Furthermore, Svevo's stage plays always have a middlebrow, melodramatic 'feel' about them, even when they are tackling social or moral issues. Rather like the dramas of George Bernard Shaw, they want, too much, to try and convince us of the significance of his characters' concerns. As a result, their psychology seems tacked on, rather than being embedded in an organic vitality. The by-now-older Zeno protagonist of *La rigenerazione*, is a pale shadow – in fact a rather unsympathetic echo – of his prototype in the novel.

Svevo's life had been as idiosyncratic as those led by any of his fictional protagonists. He had been a failed lover, but was eventually a successful suitor and husband. His marriage, like the fictional Zeno's, was to be a stroke of life-transforming good fortune, though he was in no mood to see it as such at the moment of its occurrence. Through his remarkable mother-in-law, Olga Veneziani, he suddenly found himself catapulted out of drudgery as a lowly clerk in a Trieste bank into a position of key responsibility in an important industry, with an international outreach. This startling development he wryly regarded as being symbolic of his abandonment of his artistic calling.

As the London-based businessman representing the Triestine anti-fouling marine paint manufacturers Veneziani from 1903, he was, improbably, responsible for clinching one of its most important contracts – with Great Britain's Royal Navy, which was in the process of massive expansion of its battle fleet in the face of the threat from Imperial Germany. Yet for him such a development was, as he expressed it to Livia, merely 'the end of my aesthetic dreams'. Svevo the writer was to be subsumed into the industrialist Schmitz for more than twenty years.

Yet, paradoxically, the demands of the job led indirectly to James Joyce, to the promotion of his extant novels in the literary world, and the re-ignition of his creative spirit.

His new job also involved overseeing the establishment of a London factory – demanded by the British Admiralty as a condition of the deal – to produce the paint to the Veneziani secret formula by the banks of the Thames at Charlton in South East London.

Svevo's relationship with London (recorded in *Italo Svevo's London Writings*, ed. and tr. John Gatt-Rutter and Brian Moloney, 2003) was to be a love-hate affair at first. His initial verdict, 'Splendid, colossal, appalling!' held the upper hand for some time. He could not abide the bitterly cold winters and poorly heated houses which compelled him often to wear outdoor clothes in bed. Like most visitors he never came to terms with what the English are pleased to call coffee. He found the commercial and administrative classes stilted in their manner.

But he came to like Charlton and the 'ordinary' people he encountered in his wanderings around London's streets on foot. He became a supporter of Charlton Athletic FC, and was an avid reader of *The Times*, whose reports of criminal trials had a special fascination for him. On one occasion, having closely followed in its columns the trial of a man convicted of murder, he resolved to append his name to a petition for his reprieve signed by 50,000 people, on the score of the man's farewell letter to his fiancée, which impressed him as 'the warmest declaration of love I have ever heard'. Zeno-like, he did not get around to doing so.

When war broke out in 1914, Svevo was in Trieste. That the Austro-Hungarian Empire of which he was a citizen was now at war with the country which had been one of Veneziani's most important clients was merely one of the ironies in which this master of the absurd delighted. He remained in the city for the duration of the conflict. But from the moment Italy entered the war on the side of Britain and France in 1915, his sympathies as an irredentist – though never a particularly militant one – were instinctively with

Italy, and he went to some pains to prevent the Austrian authorities from laying their hands on the secret formula for the Veneziani paint.

By that time the London experience had already provided the impetus which led providentially to the encounter with James Joyce that was to propel Svevo on his journey towards recognition. In his early days in London Svevo had constantly struggled with his spoken English. Why, since he had had no problems with the grammatically much more complicated German, is not easy to say.

He had, from his schooldays in Germany, regarded its language as the gateway to a literary and philosophical culture he admired. It took him to Schiller, whom he spoke of as 'the greatest author in the world'; Schopenhauer, who hovers over *Una vita*; and to Freud, whom he found useful in the creation of Zeno. By contrast the English he was required to equip himself with was a specifically commercial instrument. He was too, a great admirer of Shakespeare, but he had first encountered him not in English, but in German. He had come to him through what Livia was to describe in her memoir as 'fine translations', presumably those of A.W. Schlegel, whose affinity with the spirit of their originals had led to Shakespeare's immense popularity in the German-speaking world. One has only to read the explosive opening scene of *King Lear* in Schlegel's version to feel how 'right' the language and rhythm of his German is for Shakespeare.

Svevo's pressing requirement was to acquire a working knowledge of the kind of English that would enable him to get the details of his business in London right. Misunderstandings in technical and financial issues, in such large contracts as those with the British admiralty were clearly not to be thought of. It was a stroke of sheer luck that Joyce drifted into Svevo's ken in 1907. No other man among that vagrant crowd, hawking their English teaching as freelancers in Trieste at that time, could possibly have dovetailed temperamentally and culturally with Svevo as Joyce did.

Not that Joyce was in the slightest bit likely to be of much help in instructing Svevo or anyone else in commercial English. But that minor impediment soon became irrelevant. Trieste, and its dialect, interested Joyce, who liked anything off the beaten track. Joyce soon came to find Svevo most congenial company during his visits to the large Veneziani house where he came three times a week to give him his lessons.

The cocksure Irishman, with his views on his countrymen's oppression by their English overlords that, to a certain extent, resounded with Trieste's irredentists, in his turn fascinated Svevo. The English essays he wrote for Joyce are shot through with a perceptivity about the nature of his teacher, a man like himself occupying a position somewhat tangential to the bourgeois universe. Naturally, Joyce was not above using their sessions to advance his view of himself as a great writer, and introduce evidence of what he had so far done – and further intended to do – in literature. Livia, who also took English lessons from Joyce, was so moved by his reading of his short story 'The Dead' that she impulsively gave him a bouquet of flowers she had picked from her own garden.

Eventually, these close confidences drew from Svevo the shy admission that he too, had had literary ambitions. Joyce was immediately interested. He asked Svevo to lend him copies of *Una vita* and *Senilità*. From that moment Svevo had a foot on the first rung of the ladder to literary recognition. Egocentrically certain, as Joyce was, in his own qualities, he was not blind to the merits of others. He was particularly impressed with *Senilità* which he pronounced to be a work of genius, and told its author that he was a neglected writer of stature.

Joyce, of course knew Svevo as 'Schmitz', and always referred to him as such. Only to himself was he Svevo. But in these years as a Veneziani employee, when he had outwardly abandoned the pursuit of literature, that name lay well below the visible surface of his daily life. Yet the assumption of the famous pen-name had come as early as the publication of his first novel in 1893. Until that time he had written, as a journalist, under several noms de plume, adhering to his birth initials, sometimes simply 'ES', at others 'E. Samigli'.

The search for the inspiration for his pseudonym Italo Svevo takes us further back. Clearly it reflects his consciousness of his Italian-German roots, his German school upbringing and the affinity he felt with the German authors he had read. But why, in that case call himself Svevo – that is to say 'Swabian' – when his own German ancestry was in fact rooted in the Rhine valley, and his influential German education had been in a small town on the River Main, both geographically and culturally at some remove from Swabia (*Schwaben*), a region in the extreme South West of Germany?

The answer seems to lie partly in his interest in the somewhat convoluted circumstances of the journeyings of his paternal grandfather, Adolfo Schmitz, en route to his finally settling in Trieste. Rhineland-born, Adolfo had become an Austrian government employee and at one point had worked in Treviso (then, like Trieste, a city of Austria). Later in his life he had found himself posted to the small town of Köpchen in the eastern, Transylvanian part of the Austro-Hungarian empire (now Copsa Mica in Romania), whose predominantly German settlers spoke a Swabian dialect. This, and the nickname this propensity earned the locality, as 'Schwabenland', seems to have tickled Ettore's fancy when he came to think of a pen-name that would reflect his own cultural diversity.

One might wonder, too, whether at moments he identified with another eminent Swabian-Italian, that mediaeval *stupor mundi* the Emperor Frederick II, who, besides being a soldier and ruler, was a poet, and literary pioneer in the use of an Italian vernacular romance language (Sicilian) to replace Latin as a vehicle for verse.

So much for the serpentine trail that culminates in the nom de plume which, though it was hardly ever used to identify him among contemporaries in his lifetime, was to adorn the cover of his first novel, and everything he published thereafter, ultimately to eclipse the name and family of his birth.

3

Una vita

IT IS HARDLY SURPRISING THAT SVEVO'S first proposal for a title for his first novel, 'Un inetto' (An inept man), was turned down by its eventual publisher, Vram of Trieste. It was judged that a title which advertised the novel's protagonist as a man whose character ran in direct opposition to the romantic super-hero then de rigueur in Italian literature was not likely to give the book a commercial success.

They were doubtless right. Nevertheless it is a pity. The novel's eventual Italian title, *Una vita*, led – perhaps inevitably – to its being translated into English as *A Life*, the route of least resistance, doubtless, for a translator, but a label that is somehow even more inert than it is in Italian. It completely fails to stimulate curiosity. A timely return to an English equivalent of Svevo's original label – 'The Incompetent', 'The Failure' or something like it – might perhaps succeed in making Svevo's first novel sound like what it was: a provocative, revolutionary undertaking which suggests a creative talent rich in intriguing possibilities, and which has greater kinship with the work of the Austrian Musil than with any other Italian novelist of his time.

As Brian Moloney says: 'Schopenhauer and Herbert Spencer are the unnamed but unmistakably omnipresent co-Presidents of the immortals in the world of Svevo's first fiction.' At the same time it's true only up to a point. Svevo had of course read and absorbed Schopenhauer and Spencer and was determined to translate this experience into fiction. But in truth he was no philosopher. And there is much of great interest in *Una vita* which completely eludes the domination of these two formidable influences.

As a novelist Svevo likes to *play* with his knowledge of philosophy and psychology – as he does pre-eminently in *Coscienza*. But once the creative juices are flowing his own perceptions and experience of life take over. It does not necessarily help us in deciding what sort of novel – and how successful a novel – *Una vita* is, constantly to refer its procedures and assumptions to Schopenhauer. If Svevo leans on Schopenhauer to help him out (as Joyce does with Homer in his *Ulysses*) he never allows the philosopher to usurp the role of the novelist, any more than Joyce did with the archaic Greek poet. As the critic Bobi Bazlen cautioned Montale, over the latter's over-zealous farewell to Svevo in the weekly journal *La Fiera Letteraria* in September 1928, it is dangerous to tend 'the legend of a bourgeois Svevo, intelligent, cultured, profound, a good critic, psychologist, a clairvoyant of life, etc ... All he had was genius: no more'.

And as Furbank has pointed out, the motives and manner of the suicide of the book's protagonist, Alfonso Nitti, is actually a total abnegation of the Schopenhauerian dictum of the human world as expressed in his magnum opus: *Die Welt als Wille und Vorstellung.* ('The World as Will and Idea', perhaps better translated as: 'The World as Will and Representation'). Much of what happens both inside Nitti's head and in his life read more like an ironic commentary on Schopenhauer than the actions of a disciple of the philosopher.

As Moloney stresses, it is a simplification to see the plight of Alfonso Nitti as merely: what happens when a country boy translated to a prosperous urban bourgeois commercial society tries to step beyond the bounds of his own class. For a man supposedly paralysed by self doubt Nitti actually does very well in becoming the lover of his boss's daughter at the bank in which he is a lowly clerk. Had he chosen to close with this relationship and demand of her father that he and Annetta Maller translate their affair into marriage to avoid a scandal, there is nothing that Maller senior could have done about it.

Racked as he is by criss-crossing currents of neuroses, Nitti cannot bear to settle for the obvious. He flees the scene at the very moment that he might not only have bettered himself, but also helped an old family friend, Francesca – who has become Maller's mistress – to better herself also by becoming the boss's wife. Unfortunately for Francesca, Nitti's 'love' for Annetta doesn't outlive their first night of sexual activity together, and Francesca's hopes of marrying Maller will not be realized.

Of course, as a Triestine bourgeois husband he would not have needed to let his wife's inadequacies fetter his mental processes, nor for that matter his carnal appetites which might have been alleviated by recourse to mistresses or prostitutes. The question is rather: what *are* these processes and proclivities which he seems so determined to defend even when they lead him straight to destruction?

The opening chapter, which takes the form of a letter written to his mother not long after his arrival in Trieste, sets the tone. Alfonso is dogged by those conflicting enemies of mental peace: a deep sense of social inferiority and a conviction of his intellectual superiority. A well-read man, he feels contempt for those of his bank colleagues who look down on him: 'They're just coxcombs the lot of them, who spend half their days in front of their mirrors. An ignorant lot! Why, if someone handed me any Latin classic I could comment on it all; but they wouldn't even know its name.'

This is a far cry from the intellectual superiority felt by Joyce's Stephen Hero. Nitti has none of Stephen's intellectual swashbuckle. His thin-skinned psyche is pierced by doubt at every point. It has too little fierceness in it to survive among such colleagues as he has. Almost before we have taken our first steps into this society in his company, we feel a keen apprehension about the way things are to be with him at the Maller bank.

For a man of a superior intellect Nitti seems puzzlingly incompetent at grasping the essentials of the repetitive tasks he is asked to perform at work, which are brilliantly delineated by Svevo in all their stultifying minutiae. We learn that he has at the outset been spurned by not being invited round to the Maller house, as is the custom for new employees. It's a slight that much is made of in the toadying hierarchy of the bank, personified by Luigi Miceni, who goes out of his way to rub it in. The omission is in fact later rectified by Maller who, it appears, had merely been distracted momentarily from making this formal gesture by the good fortune of some important new business that has suddenly come his bank's way. In any event, the keenly anticipated evening is not a success, and only drives Nitti further into himself. Annetta's conspicuous rudeness to him as an inferior employee does little for his fragile self-esteem.

Nitti suffers to an acute degree from the paralysing fin de siècle ennui which afflicts all Svevo protagonists. In him it reaches, at times, a state of almost complete inertia. He is quite unable to assert any of his undoubted qualities of mind either in his work or in his personal relationships within the Maller bank. There is something Kafka-esque in the morass of misunderstandings in which he becomes embroiled with his superiors, all of which are made the more intractable, both by the bank's tortuous methods of working and the labyrinthine layout of the building that houses it.

Wandering the streets at night as an escape from the dreary room he rents for a pittance in the house of the struggling Lanucci family, whose straitened circumstances make something of a subplot, Nitti embarks on a series of *corse dietro alle gonnelle* – 'skirt-chasing expeditions'. These amount to no more than following a randomly-selected woman along the streets and for the most part failing even to pluck up the courage to utter as much as a word to her. When one of these selections, to his amazement and delight, not only listens to an impassioned diatribe which amounts to a declaration of love for her at first sight, but actually agrees to a future appointment, he persuades himself that the 'evening study hours' he has reserved for self-improvement are more important, and stands her up.

At this stage in the novel an impossible chasm seems to yawn between such crippling shyness and social ineptitude and the boss's daughter's bedchamber. All he has to propel him in that direction is a dogged sexual desire which, however, he is cunning enough to translate into an appearance of infatuation for her. And Annetta, who fills her hours of boredom tinkering with literary projects, begins to show him some interest when she realizes that he is something of a 'literary man'. He allows her to badger him with demands that he publish some of his 'work' (though in fact he has to that point written nothing) and this flatters her sense of being an arbiter in literary matters.

Characteristically, in a novel which, though somewhat rough hewn, is already showing signs of the Svevian tendency to achieve its effects tangentially, the leap from this to a full-blown project to possess her as his mistress comes not from himself but from outside their relationship. He learns that Annetta's companion, Francesca, who happens to be an acquaintance of his mother's from their home village, is in fact Maller's mistress. This knowledge triggers a violent erotic reaction in Nitti. 'He felt something akin to jealousy in imagining that fair hair and white flesh thrown into the arms of that cold man Maller.'

He is seized with a conviction that all this renders Maller's daughter more accessible to him. 'For the first time he dreamt of becoming Annetta's lover. It seemed less impossible now that he saw her amid love intrigues that no one bothered to hide from her ... He did not go so far as to dream of being loved because he could not imagine an expression of affection or desire on her cold, marmoreal face. His was the dream of a vicious boy in which she abandoned herself to him coldly, for pleasure, or to revenge herself on a third person.'

Is Svevo not quite in control of his material here? This seems an astonishing quantum leap into cynical man-of-the-world thinking in a character of whom not so long before we were told: 'At twenty-two his senses had the delicacy and weakness of an adolescent's'.

The development of Nitti's character as he approaches his goal of possessing Annetta shows a man seesawing wildly between timidity and brazen boldness; between 'love' and clear-sighted dislike; between a crippling sense of social inferiority and intellectual contempt.

Her plan that they collaborate in the writing of a novel is at once the catalyst to their intimacy – and provides Nitti with the clearest demonstration he could want of their mental incompatibility. His idea, that the novel shall reflect much of his own journey as a complex and hyper-sensitive country boy finding himself transplanted to a materialistic urban bourgeois ethos, is seized upon with apparent approval by Annetta – and immediately transformed by her into a vulgar romance. '"Of course instead of a clerk we'll make you rich and noble, or rather just noble. The riches we'll keep for the end of the book.'"

Nevertheless, beguiled by the physical proximity their work involves to a young woman who moreover seems to like what this collaboration is revealing of a man whom she had previously thought of merely as an employee of her father's, he is in danger of declaring himself to her during their very first collaborative session together. Fortunately, her peremptory treatment of her father's long-standing personal messenger, Santo, as she tells him to light the gas, brings him to his senses.

Their 'creative' enterprise soon becomes a chore for him, beginning 'to take on an odd resemblance to his work in the bank. In the evening he would sit down to it with a yawn, struggling against sleep, intent only on keeping closely to what Annetta had told him to do.'

Nitti's earlier uncertainties in his approach to Annetta have by now developed into a clear-sighted assessment of precisely where her attractions for him lie: ' ... his love for her was increased by the riches surrounding her, embellishing a pretty face as a setting does a diamond ... he had been excited by knowing that she was Maller's daughter, and from that agitation had come the feeling he called love.'

His first 'declaration' comes with a stolen kiss of her hand. She doesn't seem to object. After their first full-scale kiss we are told that she eventually 'broke away from his embrace, but shaken and not at all angry, murmured gently: "Leave me, Alfonso!"'

What are we to make of her willing participation in this pre-sexual activity? Is she a calculating flirt? She is clearly aware that half her father's office is in love with her. Her cousin (and potential 'official' suitor) the lawyer Macario, is becoming jealous of Nitti and the intimacy created by their creative venture. Fumigi, one of her father's employees, proposes to her, and lies to his colleagues about his rejection. Miceni, whom Nitti particularly dislikes, tells him that Annetta is 'a vain little thing who wanted to see someone die of love for her, but had not succeeded so far'.

This may be true. The boss's daughter does seem to be causing emotional chaos among the males of Maller's firm. Whether she is absolutely under her own control in so doing is open to doubt. Her attitude to Nitti, who now claims the right to fondle and kiss her whenever he wants, on the road to becoming her lover, is a thing of fits and starts, though always underpinned by a sense of strong sexual tension. It reads like an utterly modern romance between two young people. Nothing so explicit is imaginable in an English or American novel of the same date. Nitti alternates between periods in a torture of despair and at others failing to lavish on her the attentions he knows are required. Annetta vacillates between the repulse of his advances and, at the next moment, frankly letting him know that in their limited present form they are becoming tedious.

The road to consummation is handled by Svevo with refreshing matter-of-factness. One evening Francesca sits down with Nitti and warns him with delightful frankness that his behaviour with Annetta can't escape notice for much longer: ' ... "never do that on the landing again!" she said with a laugh, threatening with a white hand the best feature in her body ... ' Notwithstanding her role as chaperone to Annetta, her advice to Nitti is frankly subversive in terms of preserving the decencies of a bourgeois family. '"Can't you see that caresses not followed up destroy all influence over us women of the men who give them?"'

This may be no more than merely well-meant advice from an older woman. But we know that Francesca has a shrewd instinct that the seduction of the daughter by Nitti and the marriage that will surely follow to prevent a scandal, will improve her chances of converting her own affair with the father into a band of gold. In any event Nitti is to have much the same advice from Annetta herself only a few days later. When he catches her alone and tries to pull her to him she rebuffs him contemptuously: "'All this constant kissing's a bore.'"

This echoing, as it seems, of Francesca's advice casts the older woman in the role of orchestrator of what follows. It's a prerequisite for Annetta that Francesca shall be out of the house not merely in another room. On the day 'it' happens, Nitti meets her coming downstairs in street clothes as he is ascending to the library. "'I'll be back in half an hour,'", she tells him, effectively allocating him his 'time slot' for the deed. 'Alfonso's legs trembled as he went on up. Would he screw up courage to do what he intended in half an hour? The action itself agitated him less than the thought of compressing it into so short a time.'

The brief paragraph in which the deflowering of Annetta is accomplished does not attempt to ape conventional descriptions of lovemaking in literature. And although she sheds a few tears and utters a prettily conventional "'My God what have we done?'" afterwards, the practical way in which she immediately tidies her disordered clothing indicates to him pretty clearly that she is far from devastated by what has happened.

On the dot of the prescribed half hour Francesca is back, guessing at once what has happened. She shows Alfonso out with 'a shake of the hand and a friendly, even respectful bow. "Honour to merit" she seemed to be saying.'

It's all very matter of fact. Alfonso descends the stairs expecting no more from the encounter. What he hasn't bargained for is that what we imagine to be (for her certainly) a fairly unsatisfactory experience of sex has bred in Annetta a desire for its immediate repetition. She is waiting for him on the landing. ' ... he knew he deserved all Annetta's possible reproofs. Instead she came towards him, her eyes without trace of tears. She had paused at the door with a finger to her lips listening for any movement in the passage, smiling like a boy hiding from someone as a game'.

It's easy to dismiss Nitti's and Annetta's affair in the terms in which he is soon afterwards to analyse it, despising the steps towards it as a farago of pretences, and disparaging both their attitudes to it as false and somehow degrading to the entire process. Sexual encounters in Svevo are never presented as tendentious Lawrentian affirmations of the physical and emotional life. But even when conducted between the old men of his later stories and much younger women, they tend, at the least, to be enjoyable. And so it is here. When, immediately after her first surrender to him, Annetta summons Nitti to bed for a whole night of passion, the story, so to speak, 'cheers up'. The neurasthenic twists and turns of the psychological narrative emerge from their dark tunnel. The protagonists of this romance (or at least the female one) begin to have fun together. Physical closeness brings out Annetta's capacity for kindness.

'She was an obliging, passionate lover. She asked him to forgive her the brusque words she had pronounced a short time before. "I did think all that but I now realize it was silly of me".' She enjoys it all, laughing out loud in naïve delight as she considers the degree to which this huge joke is 'one in the eye' for the pompous cousin Macario, whom she is expected to marry for his money.

When they eventually part at four in the morning, she enthusiastically contemplates their continuing to do what they have been doing. 'She began to laugh and with frank sensuality added: "We'll have lots of days and lots of nights together".' We find ourselves liking her the better for this.

Alas, Nitti is incapable of enjoying Annetta at the cheerful face value she places on this romp of theirs. He is scarcely down the stairs into the street before he has introduced the serpent of scepticism into this briefly established paradise. 'A white figure from Annetta's room was waving him greetings with a white handkerchief. He jerked his hat about in reply. The gesture was forced but he lacked the corresponding sensation. The sight of Annetta at the window reminded him that was the customary procedure in the game of love.'

In his conquest of Annetta he has somewhat surprisingly shown himself capable of exercising the Schopenhauerian faculty of will, a fact of which he is now keenly aware. 'Some time before Macario had told him that he was incapable of fighting and seizing his prey ... Now he had shown that Macario was mistaken.' He has certainly travelled far from the shrinking individual who joined the Maller firm to become the butt of the very meanest of his colleagues. But he is almost immediately at work to undermine in himself a consoling contemplation of this initial advance he has made towards becoming a 'successful' human being.

He first evaluates its advantages. 'Oh come! Surely this victory of his did give him liberty! Even though his affection for Annetta was not what it should be – as in parenthesis he had already confessed – with this marriage his life was just beginning and he must surely be delighted at that.'

From his advance to this point in extracting what today's sportsmen tend to term the 'positives' in any adverse situation, Nitti now embarks on a relentless undermining of himself. A letter arrives from Annetta. He opens it anticipating its containing 'the words that would free him from his torture, either new pretences of love, or laboured excuses to free herself from him'.

It doesn't. It's an affectionate repetition of the desire to continue with the 'lots of days and lots of nights together' she had looked forward to during their lovemaking. She will tell her father what has happened, and that she wants to marry him. She has a scheme for getting him out of Trieste on a business errand until the storm blows over. She fixes a place and time for a meeting before this happens. 'This letter, marked all over with strong affection, moved Alfonso, but in a completely different sense than Annetta might have hoped.'

I don't think we have to alter our opinion of what Annetta is at bottom (though she *has* actually 'improved', at least momentarily, as a result of her experience) to feel that Nitti's reaction to her letter is unjust and that his analysis of her motives is actually mistaken. 'In his eyes it seemed pointless to make all that effort to appear glad and not just resigned ... No, she had fallen and was acting like a person on the lookout for the most dignified position to fall in ... That letter, it seemed to him, showed that where sensuality stopped the behaviour dictated by reasoned necessity began.'

Is there something verging on the pathological in his suspicion of Annetta's (and Francesca's) motives? Is Annetta's plan of getting him out of town while she confronts her father merely a ruse? Has she actually no intention of telling her father anything? Or are we entitled to take her stated intentions for her and Nitti's future together at face value?

Is her whole reaction to it all to be ascribed merely to the feel of 'afterglow' in the wake of successful sexual coupling that will in due course evaporate? Francesca has already warned Nitti that there is a fundamental coldness in the Maller psyche from which Annetta is not free.

In any event her promised meeting with him never takes place. Detained by her father, she is unable to make their appointment, and sends Francesca instead. I don't think we are meant to take this merely as a deliberate delaying tactic to let her 'cool down' as it were. Francesca never hints at that – and Nitti does not assume it.

Nevertheless Francesca does bring home to him the dangers inherent in his leaving the scene, for whatever reason or length of time.

"'What sort of love do you think you've inspired in her, that of the ladies of old which resisted all obstacles and lasted for ever ... You're confident enough to leave her here exposed to her father and her relatives' advice, are you? Do go if you want to, and return after only a week. You'll find yourself just a little quill driver at the Maller bank again and Annetta won't even remember she ever knew you ...'"

Nitti has been going through a convoluted series of arguments to himself during this encounter. He's alive to the personal motive in Francesca's vehement advocacy. This momentarily turns him into a prig who tells Francesca that he will acquiesce in whatever Annetta wishes, 'most scrupulously'. As to her blunter question: does he think Annetta will remain faithful to what has happened, he replies in a pompous parody of the wedding vows, "'I do'".

It's a characteristically Svevian mental evolution. He is in fact highly sceptical of what he asserts. But, in his mind, 'It was a good solution because, while before he had feared being forced into the part of betrayer, now he became the betrayed with no other obligation than to grant a generous pardon, which was easy and agreeable to do.'

This psychological ruse, this piece of deliberate repositioning of Nitti's motives, would not be out of place in *La coscienza*. But as he leaves Trieste, Nitti's reflections feel less surely grounded in the realities of the world he inhabits. 'He was fleeing from Annetta, the girl who had given herself to him from adolescent curiosity, and was persecuting him with her artificial love; but he breathed freely also at leaving all the people, bad or unlucky, among whom he had been forced to live. Francesca who had yielded to Maller because he was rich and, astute simulator that she was, hid an iron will and clever intrigues to raise herself ... that dreary Lanucci home where he felt so wretched amid all their troubles ... what dreary, squalid people!'

We are able to admire the sophistication, if you like, of Nitti's plan to present himself as the jilted party in his relationship with Annetta. But this high-handed condemnation of a raft of desperately unfortunate characters who do at least provide him with an affordable roof over his head, comes over as self pity of a far less attractive kind.

Svevo was to admit on at least one occasion in later life that as *Una vita* progressed he felt that he had lost control of the character of its protagonist. We might say, and not only of the character, but of the whole novel, which becomes inordinately diffuse at the very moment it needs to be concentrating on its aims. Up to this moment *Una vita* has had a psychological tension to hold it together. Once Nitti has come to his resolution of wanting to be 'ditched' by Annetta, this is fatally dissipated.

There are still many good things to come in the book. It is characteristic of Svevo that his protagonist should make his excuse for leaving the city a fictional illness of his mother's, only to get home and find that she is in fact dying.

Critics have disagreed on the merits of the scenes associated with the illness and death of Nitti's mother. It seems to me that they are actually rather good – one of the best things in the book. Svevo does deathbeds well, both here and in *Senilità* and *La coscienza*. He never falls victim to the kind of mawkishness and sentimentality – and psychological untruth – that for, example, Dickens does on such occasions.

Nevertheless the removal of Nitti from the centre of the book's action for a substantial interval, with a third of the book still to run unbalances it, substituting for the psychological tension already established in his city existence a whole new set of issues for him. It is not that these issues are of themselves unimportant. Svevo (and Nitti) have no intention of glorifying the 'truth' of village and country family life at the expense of the city rat race. The so-readily peddled view of the superiority of Italian family life – in particular, care for their elderly – to that of northern cultures is mercilessly exposed.

Nitti arrives at his mother's house to find her gravely ill, but being tended to in an atmosphere of carelessness and neglect. No one has even bothered to open a window to let some fresh air in to ameliorate the unwholesome miasma of the sickroom. Those around her, who include a slatternly hired carer, family friends and the incompetent local doctor, are cruelly indifferent, self-obsessed and self justifying, concerned only with their self-importance and not at all with alleviating the sufferings of the dying woman. Nitti is so upset that he bursts into tears.

It's a movingly observed moment in Svevo's presentation of a character who, whatever else his interest for us, does not often in *Una vita* arouse our deepest sympathy. Whatever else Nitti may prize about his conduct in this mess of a life of his, his care for his mother is one of the most attractive aspects of him displayed in the book. His mother's reciprocal interest in, and care for him and his 'affair of the heart', as she conceives it from the depths of her bed of pain, seem to ratify it. When she catches him with tears in his eyes on receipt of a letter from Francesca which warns him of his peril, in relation to Annetta, we honour her concern, even though we know she is completely wide of the mark on the real reasons for his fit of emotion. It's an episode that lives powerfully on its own merits, escaping completely any Schopenhauerian prescription, or indeed any other intention Svevo might have had, for it.

Intentionally or not, he makes something dignified of the passing of this now mere husk of a human being in all the ghastliness of her bedsores and suffering, and the stupidity of the carer who suddenly takes it upon herself to think she can keep her alive simply by holding her in her arms. 'Perhaps the sick woman felt the nearness of death because, raising her head as if wanting to greet it courteously, she murmured, "This I've never felt." They were her last words.'

Not even the pomposity of the doctor who arrives immediately after the event, still determined to conduct 'a careful examination, as if it were a question of remedies', can detract from this moment of tender calm amid human idiocy. But such moments of vivid compassion surface only fitfully in *Una vita*. It's almost as if they happen in spite of, rather than because of, Svevo, who by this stage really only wants to get Nitti back to the city to work out for him the fate that inevitably awaits him as a result of his management of events.

In his absence Annetta has become engaged to Macario. "'I am charged by Annetta to tell you to forget her; she will do the same'", Francesca tells him bluntly. And her analysis of his motives for behaving as he has, with the result she predicted, is the right one: "'You were escaping the consequences of your good luck.'" She has, in a sense, identified the Zeno-esque characteristics belonging to the protagonist of a novel that has yet to be written. Her bitterness at the outcome: "'My chief consolation in my misery is knowing that you're miserable too'", isn't something we can reproach her for. Nitti has ruined her life, when he might have helped her into prosperity at no cost to himself, as she sees it.

Events are now to present him with the opportunity of making amends in an act of charity for another young woman 'in trouble'. The subplot of Nitti's relations with the Lanucci family, with whom he lodges – on hold while he has been away in his home village – is now resurrected by Svevo. Signora Lanucci has from the outset seen him as a husband for her daughter Lucia, a plain young woman without any mental qualities to attract him.

We sympathise with her mother, preposterous though her hopes are. With a ne'er-do-well son and a husband incapable of contributing to the family economy, she is constantly and desperately seeking some way to sustain them in conditions just above absolute poverty. When it becomes clear that Nitti is not to be the man who will do that, the addresses of another suitor, Mario Gralli, an overseer at a printer's, are accepted by Lucia and her eager mother.

On his return to town Nitti learns that Gralli has jilted Lucia, but not before making her pregnant. A pregnancy of this sort in an English or American novel of the period would have a breathless silence enshrouding it, created by the weight of society's disapproval. Not here. There is a robust vociferousness about the response of those considering themselves to be of the injured party. Signora Lanucci is not at all in the mood to be secretive about her daughter's misfortune. Nitti has scarcely got through the Lanuccis' front door before he is made master of the details, in spite of her husband's attempts to hush her up: "'We've only had to put up with poverty so far, now we have dishonour, too ... I'm to be a grandmother.'"

We are very much in *verismo* territory here. Svevo handles family threats of *vendetta* against the seducer, like a veritable Verga – though there is nothing here of Verga's sombre tone and outlook, or the linguistic resources that made the Sicilian writer able to employ the vernacular of peasant life to make that life so vivid.

There is to be no tragic *cavalleria rusticana* here; instead the canny commercial calculations of the city's lower classes.

The episode is shot through with low but robust comedy. We have farcical boasts from the invalid Lanucci senior: "'If I were a fit man'", he cried, "'I'd go to the seducer, take him by the scruff of the neck and force him to restore the honour he's stolen from my daughter.'"

Lucia's brother Gustavo is sent in pursuit of Gralli by Signora Lanucci, who to Nitti's despair, looks forward to the violent humbling of the offender, a diminutive individual, by her broad shouldered, burly offspring. Signora Lanucci is exultant at a turn of events from which Nitti anticipates only disaster: ' ... she cried that they could not be made to accept the offence quietly and that it would be a good thing if Gustavo killed the betrayer; she would not regret his action even though it cost him twenty years in jail'.

Nitti need not have worried. When Gustavo eventually catches up with Gralli, vengeance for a sister's dishonour is easily forgotten by her brother after he has been stood a few drinks by her seducer. Nitti, sent in pursuit of the errant Gustavo, manages to persuade him to go home. As he takes over the drink-lapsed negotiations with Gralli he begins to glimpse an idea of 'doing good' for Lucia; of in some way redeeming himself in her mother's eyes for his inability to love and want to marry her himself, by using his own money as a dowry.

Gralli is soon in a way to change his mind about abandoning Lucia as he begins to sense a financial bargain in the offing. As Nitti discovers: ' ... this was a workman who knew his sums.' He has little difficulty in driving Nitti, a man now desperately anxious to do some good, up to seven times his opening offer.

There is actually a good deal going on in these last few pages of the novel. And most of it is intrinsically and vividly interesting.

But Svevo is hastening towards its end and gives the impression of impatience with the task of working out these various threads. There is the delicious irony of Nitti's being robbed of the credit for his generosity by the Lanucci family. When he returns to the house to break the good news he finds himself virtually cold-shouldered. The drunken Gustavo has regaled the family already with a completely fictitious version of his own meeting with Gralli, attributing to it a success that has both mother and daughter in ecstasies.

The conversion of Nitti's disappointment into, first, an almost masochistic delight of the abuse of his generosity ('every cold word from the Lanuccis gave him a little stab of satisfaction because on realizing how unjustly they had treated him their gratitude would be the greater') and then a pretence, to himself and Gralli, that he had intended it to be kept a secret anyway, is rather rushed past us. A Svevo in less of a hurry would have dilated on the detail of this with pleasure.

When Lucia learns what the actual price of Gralli's 'love' for her is, and who has paid it, and actually has the courage to repudiate it, Alfonso is left trying 'to convince her that Gralli was better than she thought and that he wanted money only so as to enjoy it with her'. But his kindly efforts are counter-productive. ' ... he realized that he was making no real effort to turn away a new and gentle affection for himself born in the girl's heart ... ' In what for a brief moment becomes, in spite of himself, a scene of genuine tenderness he rejects her proffered kiss on the hand as thanks, but instead 'drew her to him and kissed her on the forehead, while the girl trembled in his arms.' For her, perhaps, it's something of a consolation prize, but it's one that does not disparage her in our eyes. It is as if Svevo had witnessed or experienced such a tender moment as this in his own life, and could not bear not to put it in his novel. Like the episode of Nitti's mother's death, it happens almost in spite of him.

Which is of course, one of the drawbacks of *Una vita*. It is not a largely enough conceived novel to be able to digest quite such a ragbag of emotions and insights as it presents us with. Quite apart from the fact that fascinating characters such as Nitti's bank colleague White and his mistress drift tantalizingly in and out of it, leaving us wanting to know more, the switch-backing of Nitti's feelings, particularly in this incident-crowded last few chapters makes it difficult to follow him in his resolutions. He comes over at various moments in completely different and often contradictory guises: as naïve and totally inexperienced; as triumphantly aware of certain powers he can deploy to get his way; as philosophically detached and penetrating; as lacking in any sense of self-worth and borne down by the attitudes of inferiors; at times scorned by women; and at other moments highly attractive to them.

The ending of the book is problematical. Whether we take Nitti's suicide as a working out of Schopenhauer's notion of the world as 'performance' or 'charade', or as a critique of it, the abrupt conclusion has a perfunctory quality. We want to know more about the thought processes of the Annetta he – and we – became so close to at the height of their affair, as she apparently turns her back on that experience. But Svevo makes her allow Francesca to do her talking for her, and we can never be quite certain of the impartiality of the messenger. At the end it's asking a lot of us to accept that Annetta has actually sent her brother out into the town solely to get into a clumsy street brawl with Nitti, which will lead to a duel in which Nitti will certainly be killed.

The end feels patched-up. Nitti's rapid mental journey from accepting the probability of a humiliating death in a duel to the conviction that the better recourse is killing himself simply doesn't convince. 'Suicide would give him back Annetta's affection. Never had he loved her as he did at that moment ... Once he had vanished Annetta would no longer feel disgust born of fear at the thought of him ... He did not want to live on and appear to her as a contemptible enemy whom she suspected of trying to harm her and make her pay a high price for the favours she had accorded him.'

This is a noble resolution. But we can't help doubting that the rapid transition it represents from his previous scepticism about everything to do with Annetta, even at the height of her sexual attraction for him, would really have proceeded from a mind such as Nitti's. By contrast, the chilly letter setting out the circumstances of his death to the village notary, which ends the novel, captures absolutely the management ethos of the Maller Bank.

Una vita is nevertheless a remarkable work, in spite of its flaws in organization and balance. In my opinion its moments of greatest psychological truth and humanity arise from scenes in which Svevo forgets what he owes to his master Schopenhauer and functions simply as a realist – or if you like, a Naturalist (in the sense that both the 'weak and poor' Nitti and Francesca are defeated by the forces of wealth and power).

When his admirer Ilya Ehrenburg described Svevo as a 'Boeotian' we are not, I think meant to infer a dull-wittedness of a kind that the 5th-century BC Athenians ridiculed in their near neighbours, but merely that his intelligence was not that of the salon sophisticate, but of ordinary life lived in common circumstances. Svevo was undoubtedly in love with the idea of philosophy, but he used Schopenhauer somewhat approximately as he later, in *La coscienza*, used the theories of Freud. *Una vita*'s most vivid moments are not philosophical speculations, but shine out in the pity in the death of a neglected old woman; the petty jealousies of mentally impoverished clerks; the keen observation of the self-deceiving members of an impoverished household as it brawls its way to a solution of sorts to an inconvenient pregnancy in the family; and the final moment of tenderness between Nitti and the pregnant girl herself.

4

Senilità

JAMES JOYCE THOUGHT *SENILITÀ* SVEVO'S BEST novel. Most readers and critics haven't agreed with him, though Eugenio Montale, another of his early admirers, did. Joyce also gave the book the title by which it has become best known in English, *As a Man Grows Older.* Joyce could see that the direct rendering of the Italian as 'Senility', simply wouldn't have worked in English – would in fact have conveyed something different from what Svevo intended.

A Yale University Press edition of a new translation by Beth Archer Brombert published in 2001, was entitled *Emilio's Carnival.* This reverted to Svevo's own original suggestion for the novel's title, *Il carnevale di Emilio*, which was ignored by its first publisher, again Vram of Trieste.

The Yale Press title doesn't really work either. There is little of the colourful, outgoing atmosphere of the Italian festival of Carnevale about this intensely introspective novel – though we might of course take such a title metaphorically and make it stand for Emilio's eventual leave-taking of the fleshly delights of the world in his final banishment of his sensual mistress, Angiolina, from his life.

Joyce's title is far from ideal – though he was rather proud of it. It's rather long-winded. Perhaps something along the lines of *The Senile Soul* might have been better. For the notion of *Senilità*, as Svevo intends it, stands not simply for the age-related decline of the mental faculties, to which human beings are increasingly exposed as we live longer. It signifies, rather, the mental enervation to which its protagonist Emilio Brentani and his sister Amalia are so frequently in thrall. The notion extends to a general world weariness that seems to afflict almost all the characters in *Senilità*. Indeed, the very fabric of the Trieste society in which the book is set, is depicted as an ageing, ill-functioning affair. It is among other things riven with social injustice over which its bourgeois males preside, patronising the mistresses they take from a social stratum beneath them.

Senilità is immediately felt as a quantum advance from *La vita* in both its organization, and the depth of its characterization. Its Trieste is a more spacious place than that of its predecessor which consisted of little more than the airless rooms of Maller's bank and Nitti's threadbare digs.

Its cast of characters is much smaller, and better managed by Svevo. Through them he is able to beat a surer path through his plots, the passion – and fantastic self delusion – of Brentani's affair with Angiolina, and the equally self-delusional love of his terminally-sick sister Amalia for his mentor and friend, the sculptor Stefano Balli.

It is still fundamentally a 'realistic' novel in the well-practised convention of 19th-century Naturalism. Though there is much in it that might hint at the future existence of Zeno – exemplified in its protagonist's instinctive preference for lies over the truth – it has not yet broken the bounds of the novel as *La coscienza* does. Zola might (just) have written it. He could not have written its successor.

We don't know much about Ettore Schmitz's relationship with the alluring beauty Giuseppina Zergol, on whom he based Angiolina, beyond what he told his friend the journalist Silvio Benco. Svevo's wife Livia has seen to that, though of course the affair did not take place 'on her watch' but in Svevo's bachelor days. Zergol is briefly alluded to as part of her husband's past in Livia's memoir, *Vita di mio marito*. She is summed up in two sentences as 'a blossoming working-class girl called Giuseppina Zergol who had ended up as a circus rider. She was the first to read the part of the novel in which she appeared.'

This last throw-away piece of information does not seem to strike Livia as rather strange; as being a most interesting attention by the author to the object of an apparently unimportant dalliance – quite apart from its being an unconscious acknowledgement of her literacy, not a thing to be assumed in girls of her station in life.

In its translation into fiction in S*enilità* we are launched into the heart of an affair which is anything but a dalliance. It burns a hole in the page. From the very moment of her appearance Angiolina's effect on Brentani strikes us with well-nigh physical impact. It is clear that in Svevo's emotional development Zergol was one of the transfiguring occurrences of his life. The jealous sufferings he related to Benco as he shivered at night in the street outside her house in the freezing blasts of the Triestine *bora*, wondering with whom she was enjoying sexual intimacy inside its walls, are rehearsed vividly again as Brentani gradually becomes aware of what the life of his 'Ange' – as he insists on calling Angiolina – really is.

The novelist Svevo did not – did not want to, perhaps – return to that unvarnished realism in his dealings with women in *La coscienza*. As a writer he never again attempts such a grand passion.

That is not to say that he does not, almost to the end of his creative life, retain a high level of interest in men's – particularly old men's – sheer susceptibility to women, especially younger women, in all circumstances. But he is always able to preserve an ironical, self-mocking, distance in which the passion, such as it is, remains on a purely physical level.

The way in which Angiolina Zarri arrives in the pages of the novel prepares us for her development as Svevo's most compelling female creation. As a literary femme fatale she ranks with Zola's Nana and Alphonse Daudet's Sappho. She is one of those women whose mere proximity exercises a keenly-felt erotic attraction for men. We feel the pulse of her presence on our very first encounter with her.

At the outset of their affair the sexually inexperienced Emilio Brentani, whose sole claim to notice is the publication of a single novel printed on bad paper which has already 'turned yellow on the shelves of the bookshops', imagines that it is he who is dictating the terms of their relationship. It is, he loftily assures her, not to become *troppo seria*. It will be *facile e breve* – a 'brief and easy intrigue, such as he had so often heard described'. He likes her but she will always remain to him nothing more than *un giocattolo* – a plaything. These light-hearted proceedings, as he thinks of them, will inevitably play second fiddle to his more serious preoccupations. These are his 'career' (a lowly position in an insurance company that barely provides him with a living wage) and his 'family' (an etiolated younger sister 'who made no claims on him either physically or morally').

Angiolina says nothing to these presumptions. But her creator brilliantly expresses her sense of their fatuity, without confiding to us so much as a word on the subject. All he has to do is to depict her walking beside Brentani as he proses on, 'a tall healthy blonde with big blue eyes and a supple, graceful body, an expressive face and a transparent skin glowing with health'.

Svevo does not strain to add extra charge to this description of her – he never does. But we are left with the deep impression that Brentani, for all his *doveri* (duty) and his *famiglia*, is ripe to drop them in a moment when confronted by those irresistible fleshly splendours walking at his side.

Only after their first meeting has established a momentum to their intimacy do we learn that it is Angiolina, in fact, who has brought it about. While out walking she has adroitly dropped her sunshade, furnishing Brentani, whom she knows is coming up behind her, with a pretext for accosting her. And when, on their first real 'date' a few days later, he is so overawed by her physical presence close to him that 'he would have been content just to gaze at her and dream', she is determined to speed things up. His fanciful compliments on her good looks are no use to her. 'She remained thoughtful for a few moments, and then complained that one of her teeth was aching. "This one," she said, opening her delicious mouth for him to see, and displaying her red gums and strong teeth, which seemed like a casket of precious gems chosen and set there by the incomparable artificer – health. He did not laugh but gravely kissed the mouth she held out to him.'

Elizabeth Schächter's commentary on this first kiss in her book *Origin and Identity: Essays on Svevo and Trieste* (2000), with its suggestion that Angiolina's mouth, thus described, 'can perhaps be perceived as an image of the *vagina dentata* which ensnares and destroys its victims', is somewhat startling. Yet there is something in the episode that recalls Pierre Besukhov's utter helplessness in the toils of Helene's physical proximity in Tolstoy's *War and Peace*.

There are two distinct viewpoints on Angiolina within the narrative here. That of Brentani, not at all an accurate observer, and that of the author, who is here – as he never is as the Zeno narrator of *La coscienza* – for once a reliable witness. Significantly, Svevo achieves this without offering anything we might term an editorial opinion on Angiolina. Yet he makes her vivid and admirably true to herself, even in the moments of her greatest shallowness and vulgarity.

Angiolina does not get much quarter from the (predominantly male) critics. The back-page blurb to the original Penguin edition (1965) of de Zoete's fine translation rather obviated further judgment by introducing her as the 'sluttish mistress' of Brentani's 'small-town Dante'. For the American Beno Weiss (in his book *Italo Svevo*) she is 'a knowledgeable working-class girl of doubtful respectability' (a quaintly coy verdict for a man writing in 1987). And Weiss appears to approve of Brentani's friend, the sculptor Stefano Balli, for recognizing her 'as the slut she is'. From what transpires we may very much doubt that it's what Balli actually thinks of her. In any event, it's a harsh condemnation of someone who is compelled by poverty to do what she does. Why, in any event, should Angiolina's enjoyment of sexual activity be held against her? Schächter asks, in inviting us to admire in her, as she believes Svevo does, 'the power and energy of female sexuality'.

Svevo makes absolutely no comment. He allows her to be judged, as women in her circumstances are in Svevo's Trieste, by the men who exploit them. These men seem resolutely to ignore the fact that these favours are being granted by a class of woman who has no choice in the matter if she wants to put bread in her mouth and of those who depend on her.

The grinding poverty to which an 'honest' trade (such as darning worn clothes) would condemn Angiolina is everywhere emphasized. Her home is a desperately wretched place, 'mean and poverty stricken'. Angiolina, with her health and beauty, is its only meaningful source of support, through the uses to which she puts these assets, for a mother ground down by physical toil to a premature old age, a sick father who cannot work, and a sister of ten years old who, tellingly, when she answers the door to Brentani on his first visit 'did not seem at all surprised to see a new face; she only lifted her hand to her bosom to hold together her ragged little jacket, from which all the buttons were missing'.

Later in the book, when she thinks Brentani has broken up with her elder sister, this ten-year-old will try to insure herself against the probable loss of future visits from him by flinging her arms round his neck and covering his face with 'kisses that were by no means childish'. It's a moment that disgusts Brentani, who can't see beyond this 'shocking' promiscuity to the child's instinctive recognition that the household is going to need another breadwinner to bring in more visits from men.

For the moment, Brentani of course might offer Angiolina a way out of her situation. But his 'love' for her is not, of course, of the sort that has marriage in view, though it is proprietorial enough to make him indignant when he learns that she is deceiving him with other men. Before this dawns on him he persists in his delusion that the 'amazing purity of her profile and her incomparable health' are somehow safeguards against a corruptible nature.

Decades later in Svevo's creative life we find his philandering protagonists still approaching their quarry with this *mens sana in corpore sano* delusion. When in *La novella del buon vecchio e della bella fanciulla*, set in 1917, by which time his country is fighting against Italy, the 'nice old man' allows his gaze to play over the curving shoulders and breasts of a pretty young tram driver, he excuses himself with the fiction that 'A beautiful complexion or a beautiful line are, in fact, the expression of the highest intelligence', as a licence to seduce her.

Brentani's friend and mentor Balli, though he gives himself irritating airs on the score of his greater worldliness, has the advantage of being a genuine bohemian himself. He can see where Angiolina is coming from and cautions Brentani against her, knowing only too well his friend's naivety and capacity for self-deceit.

To do him justice he behaves considerably better than Brentani when it is his turn to have his eyes opened in a similar fashion. He too will belatedly wake up to the fact that *his* girl, Margherita, has made parallel arrangements with other men. He was at first outraged to hear of it, he confesses to Brentani. But, in the closest any of the book's protagonists come to venting a critique of the social mores within which Trieste's bourgeois men run their mistresses, he tells his friend he has discovered that she does it to provide for 'a mother and a brood of sisters all quite young'. For a moment the man about town is moved by genuine emotion. '"Just think. She has never consented to receive a single penny from me"', he tells Emilio.

The road down which Brentani is inexorably led to some comprehension of Angiolina's true modus vivendi and at the same time sucked in to accepting it in all its bald detail, is beautifully constructed as a series of creeping revelations by Svevo. Emilio cannot accuse Angiolina of trying to deceive him. Only his own obtuseness stops him from cottoning on earlier. His absurd assumption of the air of a man of the world leads him in to a world of increasingly tangled sexual arrangements and compromises without his realizing it.

At the outset she tells him she has 'no need to earn a living'. He does not ask why. An acquaintance, Sorniani, a man admittedly much given to malicious gossip, is quick to regale him with the information that Angiolina had a much earlier entanglement with an older man, Merighi, which involved her in leaving her own home for a while. 'But Sorniani might as well have talked to the winds, for Emilio was sure he knew exactly what had happened ... He felt a profound pity for her.' When he asks Angiolina about this entanglement, she does not try to retreat under a smokescreen, but is quite candid about an arrangement that was intended to end perfectly respectably in marriage, until she, so she tells him, decided to break it off in the face of Merighi's mother's jealousy. '"I am very fond of him,"' she wound up, with an engaging frankness which gave a colour of sincerity to everything else she said.'

Brentani is nothing if not resolute in his determination to be completely taken in. 'Poor child! She was honest and disinterested. Would it not have been better to teach her to be less honest and a trifle more calculating? He had no sooner asked this question than he conceived the splendid idea of educating the girl himself.'

From this moment of extreme self delusion the 'experienced' Brentani is deaf to the accumulation of evidence which increasingly includes names, carelessly tossed into her conversation, of young men about town known to him chiefly by reputation. When stabs of doubt begin to come, they do so laterally, at first barely penetrating the fog of his self deception.

In his first hungry embraces with Angiolina he feels himself to be kissing 'the pure virginal moonlight'. But when that first illusion has been navigated and its content analysed he finds himself asking himself: Who had taught Angiolina how to kiss? Contemplating the practised fluency of her technique, the self-styled man of experience is brought up short with honest doubt that it could be himself 'who had initiated her into an art in which he was such a novice?'

He blurts out these doubts to her. They are received with that candour which now draws him insensibly but irresistibly in among the signposts that make intelligible the sexual landscape she inhabits.

It was of course Merighi who taught her to kiss. 'Emilio must be joking if he pretended to doubt whether Merighi would have taken advantage of his position as her fiancé to kiss her as much as he wanted.' Having arrogated to himself the mantle of a superior knowledge of the world, Brentani is forced to swallow this.

His first visit to her house only serves to compound his discomfort. Her bedroom is the only decently furnished room in this family hovel. He and we are left in little doubt that the photographs of various young men who adorn its walls are not in fact the various 'godfathers' she claims they are. In his humiliation and anger he betrays his jealousy and then wants to kiss her as if thereby to obliterate them from his thoughts. In her refusal to allow this liberty she produces a masterstroke: "'I have so many sins on my conscience already," she said very seriously, "that I shall find it very hard to receive absolution today. It is your fault that I am going to confession badly prepared.'"

Such a reaction is precisely calculated to appeal to Emilio's vanity. At the same time it allows him to wallow in that sense of wronging an innocent creature that is vital to his sustaining his illusions about her.

'A new hope arose in Emilio's breast. What a blessed thing religion was! He had banished it from his own life and deprived Amalia of its comfort, but now that he found it at Angiolina's side he welcomed it with indescribable joy. In face of an honest woman's religion all those men on the wall seemed less formidable, and as she went away he kissed Angiolina's hand respectfully, a homage she accepted as a tribute to her virtue.'

Poor Amalia. Estranged from the solace of her childhood religion. Nightly waiting for the homecoming of a brother whose news, such as it is, of the outside world is all she has to illumine the monotony of her existence, she is now painfully confronted by a man palpably in thrall to sexual desire. As he babbles about the magical atmosphere of a summer night in the public gardens of Trieste 'she divined on his lips the print of those kisses which really filled his thoughts. She hated that unknown woman who had stolen away her companion and her only comfort.' When his sister bursts into tears Emilio is only too ready to accept her apology and her assurances that she has been feeling unwell all day. '"If you are not better tomorrow we will send for the doctor"', is his myopic response to the hurt he is inflicting.

The velocity of Emilio's sleepwalk into Angiolina's toils is sketched by Svevo with a vividness that recalls Zola. On his very next visit: 'She had only just got out of bed and he took her wonderful body in his arms, and pressed it to him, still warm from sleep. He felt its warmth through her thin wrapper and had the sense of immediate contact with her naked body. The spell of religion had vanished very quickly, for Angiolina's was hardly of the quality to protect anyone who had to rely on that alone for her defence.'

It is a short step from this to his being able to entertain a proposition from her that would have revolted him from his 'Ange' only a few days before. Though he exerts a nominal pressure on her to surrender to him, in fact 'his incomplete possession gave him perfect satisfaction'. He is held back by 'lack of self-assurance and because he was afraid of being an object of derision to all those men who looked down at him from the wall'.

Within a few days she has come up with an ingenious solution that will circumvent society's and family objections to their becoming lovers: 'they must find a third person on whom to put the burden of any complication that might arise from their relationship [presumably a pregnancy], and whom it would be great fun to deceive'.

We may wonder how on earth Emilio can interpret this proposal of sexual skullduggery as 'a declaration of love for himself' or indeed how it is to function in practice. He consoles himself with the thought that there is actually little hope of finding a candidate for this proposed arrangement and that 'she gave him her love without trying to bind him and without endangering his independence'. She of course can have no idea that a man in his position is content in such a pre-sexual love affair. In a day or two she has presented him with a solution that will save to advance their relationship to the sexual stage – she has become engaged! The tortuous logic of the arrangement, for her, is that sexual relations between her and Emilio will eventually be able to take place under the umbrella of her intimacy with this new fiancé. Emilio's presence around her and her house will not be as conspicuous as it is now, once she is a fiancée herself.

He has got nowhere near being up to speed in the development of these proposals. He is flabbergasted. 'His anguish was so acute that he remained there petrified until he heard her reminding him that he had never minded before hearing her talking about that plan of theirs. But so long as it had only been a plan Angiolina's lips had seemed to turn it into a caress.'

In his mental turmoil, the identity of Angiolina's intended (Volpini, a local tailor) is not a primary preoccupation with Emilio. She prettily deflects his sharp enquiry as to whether she loves this new betrothed. '"You love me you know, don't you? But you never admit the possibility of marrying me." He was very touched at hearing her allude to his egotism without the slightest resentment.'

It is the first instance of true perception we have had from Emilio amid the tissue of illusions he has erected about Angiolina. Even so, he has a final hurdle to surmount over this proposed triangular relationship, which he is convinced still remains in the arena of the theoretical. His introduction to the practical truths of his situation takes place after an evening in which he introduces Angiolina to Balli whose opinion of her he wants to hear.

It's a meeting that does little for his self-esteem. In spite of the presence of Balli's woman, Margherita, at the gathering, to his dismay his friend and Angiolina immediately hit it off. She loves his direct manner and his ability to appeal to her own coarseness. '"Are you really called Angiolina? A diminutive for a great strapping girl like you? I shall call you Angiolona. Perhaps only Giolona." And henceforth he always called her that, emphasizing the broad vowels to the utmost so that the sounds conveyed the maximum of contempt. Emilio was surprised that she showed no dislike for the name; she never got angry at it, and when Balli bellowed it in her ear she only laughed as if he had been tickling her.'

When they meet the following night Emilio is intending to reproach her for her levity. She is not listening. She breaks across his thoughts with the news that her engagement with Volpini will have to be a long one owing to various business arrangements of his on which their eventual marriage will be contingent. Apart from registering a certain relief, Emilio is not really concentrating on the detail. As she chatters on he is brought up short by a new development he has not considered. '"There is something else," she said softly and rather timidly. "Volpini says he can't live a year with his desire unsatisfied."'

'He understood at last. He protested that she could not expect him to consent to such a thing. But what objection could he raise?'

As he leaves her he reflects bitterly: 'Besides, this was perhaps the cure he had been hoping for. Polluted by the tailor, possessed by him, *Ange* would soon die, and he would continue to amuse himself with *Giolona*.' Brentani's education in the imperatives of her situation, and what they mean for his relations with her, has been completed in a remarkably short time.

Yet Angiolina is not at bottom a woman formed to cause men grief, though this is something that Emilio never really understands. Her vitality invites men to join in the pleasure she herself gets from the contemplation of herself, of her vitality and the promise of lovemaking. When the prospect of her meeting Balli had been first suggested to her by Emilio she was immediately intrigued by it. "'Where can he have seen me to make him want to know me?'" she wanted to know, already anticipating scenes in which she will form the centre of the drama.

In a passage of delightfully observed naivety Angiolina cannot help venting her jealousy of Margherita, who is in her mind already her 'rival' for Balli's love. The man of the world Balli knows how to keep this jealousy alive. When Emilio blunders over-eagerly into asking him what he thinks of his new love's face Balli declares "'the modelling of her nose is not perfect; the line of the lower part is very sketchy; it needs a little retouching." "Really?" exclaimed Angiolina, very much upset.' And her fulmination against 'her terrible critic' is vented to Emilio at the first opportunity: "'As if that great gawk of his was perfect!'"

There is actually nothing self centred in Balli's behaviour towards Angiolina. She is the kind of woman with whom he will always find it easy to be on good terms. And his later response to Emilio's persistent enquiry about his prospects in love: "'I knew from the first that this was not the sort of adventure for you'", is a disinterested one. Emilio needn't fear that Balli will try to make off with his mistress merely to satisfy his vanity. Nevertheless, the price he has paid to obtain his friend's verdict on Angiolina is that he is now exposed to her evident predisposition towards him. 'It was terribly painful for him to see how lightly and easily the sculptor carried off the prize which he could not win even at the cost of so much suffering.'

Balli is, to his credit, not a man to revel in this. When he becomes convinced that Angiolina is two-timing Emilio with another man in addition to her 'fiancé' he tells him that he has just seen her out with someone other than Volpini not because he has any designs on her himself, but simply as an honest attempt to extricate his friend from a relationship he feels is doing him no good. After all he has been through in terms of being prepared to share his mistress's embraces with another man, yet another infidelity is the last straw for Emilio, particularly as this new 'rival' is a lowly *ombrellaio*. As he goes home he rehearses the indignant speeches he will reproach Angiolina with when he next sees her: '"There was no need to have me chased from my post by an *umbrella maker*." He repeated this short sentence several times, altering a word here and there and trying to perfect the tone of his voice, which became each time more bitingly ironical.'

This is characteristic Svevian comic scepticism. We doubt very much whether this new-found resolve will survive his next contact with the love goddess herself. As it happens fortitude is forced on Emilio from another quarter. After getting home, on his way to bed he passes Amalia's room and realizes she is talking in her sleep. At first his inclination is to carry on to his own, but something about her tone makes him return to her door. 'There was no connection between the separate words, but there could be no doubt that she was talking to someone she loved very much. There was a great sweetness both in the sound and the sense ... He stood there a long while listening. Just as he was going away again, a complete sentence arrested him. "Everything can be allowed on a honeymoon." Poor girl. She was dreaming of getting married.' Emilio's neglect of this fragile, isolated spirit is borne in on him. He returns to his room, full of resolve.

'Once his relation with Angiolina was broken off he would be able to devote himself wholly to his sister. He would live for duty alone.'

We have witnessed the unequal struggle between the pull of Angiolina and Brentani's sense of duty and family before. It is not of course going to be as easy as that. But Angiolina and her family help his resolve in their sheer barefaced duplicity. For once Emilio holds his nerve. The scene is beautifully observed by Svevo.

When he goes to Angiolina's next day she is out. His enquiries elicit from her mother the lie that she was out 'late' with Volpini. Emilio, who knows that the tailor is out of town mentions this but is corrected by the adjusted lie that Volpini had missed his train and was able to be with Angiolina for that evening. Angiolina returns. When they are left alone she continues with her mother's fiction, even embellishing it with plausible psychological detail. This includes a re-enactment of her fancied indignation against Volpini for detaining her for an extra evening when she thought he had gone away. At the end of her recital she has the cheek to demand a kiss. For once he is proof against her power.

'"I shall never kiss you again," he replied quietly, his eyes fixed on those red lips which he was renouncing for ever.'

Realising she has been rumbled she immediately apologizes to him for hiding behind the absent Volpini. She was of course chaperoning her friend Giulia who was out on a date with the man who was seen with them, a man who is '"head over heels in love with her; even more than you are with me."'

This winsome fabrication likewise falls on deaf ears. 'She stopped short. She saw by the look on his face that he did not for a moment believe her, and it was mortifying to her vanity to have told him two such patent lies.'

There is a certain sympathy from Svevo here in his description of the strain Angiolina suffers, caught up in her tangled web of lies. Completely at sea, now, in the presence of a man with whom previously she has called all the shots, she is observed by Svevo violently gripping the back of an adjacent chair as if letting go of it might lead to her collapse, while her face is devoid of all expression as she gazes fixedly at a stain on the wall.

Emilio stands firm, and in this he surprises us. Only a somewhat pompous (and, given the facts of the situation, preposterous) analysis of his feelings spoils his farewell. '"I loved you very much and that alone ought to have given me the right to be treated differently. When a girl allows a young man to tell her he loves her she belongs to him and is not free to do as she likes."'

Nevertheless, as Svevo allows (or is this partly Emilio's perception, too?), 'This phrase was rather feeble, but it expressed exactly what he wanted to say, which is a great deal to expect of a lover's reproach.'

The terms of their parting are at once vivid and, as one would expect with Svevo, shot through, especially on her side, with ambiguity. 'He went away, though not without having admired her one last time.

'As she stood there all pale, her eyes wide open, half from fear and half, perhaps, from doubt as to whether to tell him another lie and try to make him stop with her.'

At the point when he finally turns his back on her she gives vent, so Svevo tells us – this cannot be merely wishful thinking from Emilio – to a *suono d'angoscia* ('anguished cry'). He does not complacently chalk this up as a victory, but is genuinely curious about the quality of her grief – and we like him the better for it. We are curious too. Given the calculating nature of her previous mendacity how are we to interpret this? Merely as a reflex reaction to the suddenness of the rupture, rather than a deeply felt grief at the collapse of a treasured relationship? Or is the removal from her life of someone who is after all out of the sphere of tailors and umbrella makers, a loss she feels from a status point of view? She has certainly never treated him as if that were so. From the purely financial point of view, the socially meanest of her suitors seems more readily able to put his hand in his pocket for her on a night out. Be that as it may, her grief continues to haunt him. 'When Emilio found himself out in the road again alone, with Angiolina's cry of anguish still in his ears, it was all he could do not to return to her on the spot.'

At this juncture Emilio is clearly not out of danger. How could he be? His old acquaintance Sorniani is on hand to administer a more complete antidote to his infatuation. We sense Svevo's enjoyment of the novelist's licence as he throws the inveterate gossip across Brentani's path at the very moment when, unable to face home and Amalia, he is allowing himself to wonder whether he might not run into Angiolina on the Corso.

Sorniani is, rather like Jane Austen's Mrs Elton, one of those provoking spirits who instinctively knows how to touch others on the raw and bring them down to his level. Seeing his haggard face, he immediately pretends to think that Emilio is not well. When Emilio is glad to take refuge in this fiction, rather than confess a broken heart, Sorniani adopts more direct tactics. '"How is your love-affair getting on?" Emilio pretended not to understand. "Which love affair?" "Why, that blonde, Angiolina." "Ah yes," said Emilio casually. "I broke with her long ago."'

This assumed casualness turns out to be fatal to his composure. He is immediately heartily congratulated by Sorniani. '"She wasn't the sort of woman for a young man like you, especially if you're so delicate. She sent poor Merighi quite off his head, and since then half the town have amused themselves with her."' (In Svevo's Italian:

'*s'è fatta sbaciucchiare da mezza città*', the delightful Italian verb suggesting promiscuous kissing and probably best rendered in today's vernacular as something like 'She's let half the city snog her' – a translation of Sorniani's coarseness that wouldn't have come naturally to de Zoete in 1932.)

Emilio now has to drink even more deeply of the cup of humiliation as Sorniani parades before him 'the list of names which Brentani already knew, from Giustini to Leardi, all of whose photographs he had seen displayed to so much advantage on the wall of Angiolina's bedroom'. This recital is, infuriatingly for Brentani, punctuated by unctuous enquiries after his health from his tormentor who is all the while gleefully scrutinising his violent changes of complexion.

When Sorniani eventually departs, he does not spare himself. 'They had all possessed her except himself ... But it was not only the fact that he had never possessed her that tormented him. Up to that moment he had found comfort in the cry of anguish which he had caused her to utter. But what could a cry like that signify in the life of a woman who had experienced far greater delight as well as far greater pain in the arms of others?'

This self-excoriating immersion in sexual humiliation is not over. There is yet further to go before he has plumbed the depths of his self loathing. He has hardly got Sorniani out of his hair when he encounters Leardi himself, the 'tall, strong, handsome youth, so fair and boyish in complexion, so virile in body ... ' He suddenly can't stop himself from babbling about Angiolina to a man who has very different things on his mind. Leardi wants only to show off by talking about the poverty of social and cultural life in Trieste. He is astonished when Brentani blurts out 'Do you know Signorina Zarri?'

Evidently surprised that Brentani should even know her, Leardi admits that he knew her very well in former times when he was a friend of Merighi. Completely out of control of his emotions now, Brentani chooses to interpret Leardi's *molto bene* as having a sexual connotation and indiscreetly blurts out this suspicion. Like him, we don't believe Leardi's indignant denial.

It scarcely matters. Brentani hastily absents himself from yet another scene of torment, grinding his teeth in insane rage, as he rehearses his acute imaginings of his failure and humiliation. 'It is the wealth of images in my brain that makes me inferior,' he writhes in self-excoriation. 'If for instance Leardi had thought that Angiolina was betraying him, he would have been incapable of representing her to himself in an image as full of colour and life as he himself did when picturing her with Leardi. Why, directly the naked body was uncovered which he had only dreamed of, the commonest porter would find immediate satiety and peace of mind. It was a short, brutal act: a mockery of all his dreams, of all his desires.'

In his mental turmoil Emilio finds it difficult to adhere to his generous resolution towards Amalia. When he arrives home he shouts at her for not having lunch ready. He tries to make it up by suggesting that she goes out on such a lovely day. But what is intended as being a concern for her health comes out only as hectoring. When she silently leaves the room he is angry afresh: 'Surely I am wretched enough? She ought to have understood the state of mind I am in. My kind suggestion that she should go out ought to have been enough to make her be nice to me and not go on distressing me with her resentment.'

And so it goes on. Tossing and turning on his bed of mental pain Emilio veers between extremes of impatience and considerate affection in his relationship with his sister. Almost everything that he does returns him to the conundrum which pursues his waking hours and ruins his sleeping ones. 'Why did I, in fact abandon

Angiolina?' is simply a version of that question which pursues every man of imagination who finds that he has reduced what he would have liked to conduct as a relationship between minds to an enslavement by sex.

Do the creaking mechanics of Svevo's novel impinge here? Not to its detriment, I think. The exit of Angiolina from the plot serves to give space for the character of Amalia to develop in front of us. This is hardly likely to happen as long as Angiolina is in the vicinity. From being an utterly passive receptacle, like Shakespeare's Silence in *King Henry IV, Part II*, an almost dead moon circulating on the extreme edge of the universe of human society, she becomes a focus of sympathy and powerful pity.

Balli enters the Brentani ménage as a catalyst to Emilio's recovering a degree of composure, something he achieves in spite of the latter's tendency to jealousy of him. Visiting the house daily and passing time with the brother and sister, he imports to it cheer with the spirit of mischief-making he brings with him, carelessly tearing apart reputations as if he were among intimate friends. Seen in this attractive, devil-may-care light he also almost immediately becomes the focus of Amalia's profound emotional frustration.

'Time out' from the plot's central, erotic concerns gives Svevo a chance to explore something he is actually rather good at, involvement with a character whose life lies apart from the main flow of the story – rather as Nitti's absence from Trieste and his care for his mother did in *Una vita*. In both cases we are shown a capacity for tenderness that we don't necessarily think of as being characteristic of Svevo. Such a quality was not to be a part of *Coscienza*. By the time he came to write it he had put such emotional realism far behind him.

It's easy to regard Amalia as a purely feeble, unlikeable character. Balli is at first inclined to see her purely in those terms. 'The affectionate sympathy he had always felt for Emilio increased as the latter had hoped. Poor fellow! He had to look after an hysterical sister as well.'

It might certainly be thought preposterous that Amalia should not only fall in love with Balli, but harbour a hope amounting almost to an assumption that her affection should be reciprocated. Yet Svevo does not treat the episode in a contemptuous fashion. Balli captures Amalia's affections as easily as he provoked the interest of Angiolina. But there is a world of difference between the nature of the two women's infatuation with him. Angiolina's is the simple product of intolerance of other women who come between her and any man over whom she assumes a prescriptive right. Amalia's is that lonely hunter, her heart.

The route by which we become more closely acquainted with Amalia's qualities is a complex one. I am not sure it is exactly a planned complexity on Svevo's part. The result might have been achieved more simply, but in his dogged pursuit of meaning, here, Svevo wants us not only to share Amalia's feelings but thoroughly to understand Emilio's state of mind at this point.

Emilio appears not to want to damage Amalia's comparative return to emotional contentment that Balli's presence has brought about. At the same time he does want to revenge himself on Balli for his success with Angiolina. This leads him into warning him off Amalia on the pretext that alerting him to the dangers of his intimacy (if it can be so called) with her is a way of 'pointing out to Balli that he was not the superior person he believed himself to be, nor the most faithful of friends'.

This is a perilously complicated route to achieving his (not particularly noble) end. It goes horribly wrong when he opens proceedings by telling Balli a silly lie: 'that an aged relative had stopped him that morning to enquire whether it were true that

Balli was engaged to Amalia'. Balli sees through the lie and, to his credit, actually perceives that it has its roots in jealousy of his easiness with Angiolina.'

But the damage has been done. The situation of Amalia with whom Balli's relationship, from his point of view, had been completely neutral, has been tainted. He decides to suspend his visits to the Brentani household. Evening after evening now passes without him. For both Emilio and Amalia his absence creates a huge 'elephant in the room' between them. 'It was an expectation which Emilio could not have endured himself; it needed great courage to ask nothing except the usual question: "Is not Balli coming?" There was always an extra place laid for Balli; now his glass would be slowly put away again in the cupboard which Amalia used as sideboard. The glass was followed by the cup out of which Balli was to have drunk his coffee, and then Amalia would lock the cupboard door. Her movements were calm but very slow.'

The poignancy of this erosion of illusions and the terrible restraint with which Amalia deals with it is almost unbearable. Each 24 hours in the Brentani household and this repetition of the nightly ceremony with Balli's place setting, steadily increases the tension. When Emilio can bear it no longer he resorts to what he thinks will effect a swift cure on her. In fact it's another silly lie and just as counterproductive as the one he told Balli.

'"Do you know," he said, "what has made Balli change towards you? Someone asked him in front of me whether he intended to get engaged to you."'

We like Amalia the better for her reaction to this. Emotionally overwrought she may be, but she is not vain. We think she probably doesn't believe him. We admire the dignity with which she reacts, after the first shock has forced a burst of incredulous, dry mirthless laughter from her. '"I admit," she went on, her admirable strength of will enabling her finally to speak in a tone of real indifference, "I admit that Balli's company was not unpleasant to me, but it never occurred to me that it could be so dangerous as all that."'

When she insists that Balli resume his visits so that no credence shall be attached by the world to Balli's fears, he is in no position to refuse her since the whole episode is his fault.

To do him justice, Emilio, even though still obsessed with thoughts of Angiolina, does by now have honest, tender feelings for his sister. Restless himself in his thoughts, he pauses again at her bedroom door one night. 'But Amalia had given up dreaming; even her happy dreams had been stolen from her now. He heard her turning over and over in bed as if she did not find it very comfortable either.' He is uneasily conscious that his blundering has 'made his sister's fate more bitter'.

Emilio is at his most sympathetic as a character at this juncture in the book. But the emotional firestorm represented by Angiolina is not to leave him unscathed for much longer. Its power to diminish him as a thinking being soon short-circuits yet again his sympathy for his sister's plight.

Balli's visits are resumed. Not surprisingly in the circumstances, they are a miserable failure. He cannot create the carefree atmosphere of their first incarnation 'for he did not want to encourage her and be pestered by her falling in love with him a second time'. Amalia cannot herself respond with any spontaneity to this new, conventional Balli, boring his audience with captious criticisms of the Wagner he has just heard at the opera.

The effect of this failure is to bring home to Emilio how ineffectual his 'cure' from his enslavement to Angolina has been, and to reignite it. When he catches sight of her in the street one night he is in her toils within minutes. There is something calculatingly fetishistic in Svevo's description of the encounter: 'She was holding up her skirt to protect it from the mud, and by the light of a dim street lamp he saw the shine of Angiolina's black shoes.'

Within a short time they have progressed from polite greetings through shy reminiscences to impassioned embraces in the dark street near her house. She is not about to let him escape again. A joking reference to the 'ombrellaio' and the small matter of her having recently had to give herself to Volpini – for Emilio's sake, as she insists – are rapidly negotiated, en route to their first sexual encounter, in her bedroom practically under her mother's nose.

Yet the effect of his having had to digest her disagreeable information about Volpini before the long desired consummation, has somehow left Emilio with a form of emotional dyspepsia. He would not be the first man in those circumstances to conclude ruefully as he does: 'The male was satisfied, but beyond that satisfaction he had really felt nothing at all. He had possessed the woman he hated, not the woman he loved.'

Immediately running to unburden himself of these impressions to Balli – in spite of Angiolina's specific request not to – Emilio can find no relief for his tortured cogitations. He picks constantly at the scab of his infatuation for a woman who enthralls and repels him in equal measure. The Volpini connection torments him: 'Indeed how was it possible to explain the *fellness* [my italics - *tenacità* would perhaps have been better rendered as 'insistence', here?] with which she laid on him all the blame for her connexion with Volpini, if it were not that she intended to attach herself to him, to compromise him and to suck dry the little blood he had left in his veins? He was for ever bound to Angiolina by a strange contradiction of his own heart: by his senses (for alone in bed his desire for her had awakened again) and by the very indignation which he attributed to hatred.'

Although at the analytical level Emilio can see with admirable clarity what is happening to him, this rationale is of absolutely no help when set against the sexual manacles in which Angiolina holds him. The only resolution he can come to is: 'He could not wait; he must see Angiolina again.' To his surprise he finds her adamant that sexual activity with her at her house cannot be repeated. That is not of itself a problem. Balli has furnished him with the address of a house where rooms are let 'for a certain purpose'. He immediately goes there.

The depths to which his enslavement now drags him are laid before us in unsentimental detail. The conditions of the transaction are exemplified by the establishment's proprietor, 'a disgusting old creature dressed in a dirty garment underneath which one could divine the contours of a swelling bosom, the one vestige of youth left in her flabby old age; a few scanty curls covered her head and between them one could see her red, greasy skin'. Apart from anything else, from such unsparing detail we immediately doubt the hygiene of the place.

Its moral hygiene is quite clear, the walls are hung with photographs, 'as in Angiolina's room' . Emilio involuntarily makes the comparison, though these are not of young men but of scantily clad young women doubtless intended to serve as stimulants to jaded male appetites. In a nice touch, Svevo has a gasp of horror escape Emilio as he spots 'hanging beside the photo of a half-naked woman, a girl he used to know, a friend of Amalia's, who had died a few years ago ... '

In reply to his curiosity about this exhibit the woman tells him she has bought the pictures as a job lot to brighten the room up. The ambience of the place is at stark odds with the night of – this time, he hopes – untainted love he wants with Angiolina. There is still enough refinement of feeling left in his system not to be profoundly saddened by the presence of Amalia's dead friend in such company. As the harpy hovers about him waiting to talk terms he 'gazed for a long time at the sweet face of the poor girl who had posed before the camera all dressed up in her best – perhaps just that once in her whole life – only to serve as an adornment for that sordid little room.'

As for the tryst itself, no wonder that Joyce, who at the time he first read *Senilità* was still struggling painfully to bring his *A Portrait of the Artist as a Young Man* to perfection, so admired/envied Svevo's handling of the episode. The term 'explicit' would give the wrong impression of the treatment of the sexual encounter between Emilo and Angiolina. Svevo is not interested in merely transgressing the boundaries of polite convention in terms of physical description. This coming together is, rather, a thing of naked sexual candour unlike anything in the European novel to that point. By comparison the descriptions of couplings in the novels of Zola and Flaubert seem overwrought. And Stephen Dedalus's initiation with a prostitute in the *Portrait of the Artist* described as 'darker than the swoon of sin, softer than sound or odour', feels overdone, in Joyce's attempt to freight it with an emotional significance it can't possibly warrant.

Emilio and Angiolina lie down together in an episode of dispassionately observed realism. Emilio wants it to be a thing of passion that overwhelms any need for analysis. Only when he reflects upon it later is he made aware of the huge folly of such a desire and the completeness of his disillusionment: ' ... now he knew, knew with absolute certainty, that Angiolina had known men who had given her more pleasure. Several times she had said: "Now that is enough. I can't bear any more." She had tried to say it in a tone of admiration which she had not succeeded in finding.'

Angiolina is not a woman to get herself out of tiresome sex with feigned adoring and a faked orgasm. Emilio tries clumsily to bang his way, if not to his woman's heart at least to her erogenous core. He is simply not well enough acquainted with her physiology to know what this might be. And she feels under no obligation to expose herself to physical discomfort by submitting to excessively prolonged and unproductive sexual activity.

Equally realistic is Svevo's insight into the psychology of the man faced with these unpalatable truths, especially when he is (unlike the previously imagined 'commonest porter', unhitching his trousers, coupling brutishly with Angiolina and moving on, untouched by the experience) 'a mixture of wounded vanity and the bitterest jealousy'.

This jealousy is constantly, if all unwittingly, fanned by her behaviour as their relationship moves towards its second dissolution. By this time, convinced that her future cannot lie with his, she is becoming increasingly reckless about keeping him waiting for their assignments, while fitting in other business. As she seeks on one such occasion to 'pacify him with a few caresses', he feels the heat and smell of a recent sexual encounter on her as she flings her naked arms round his neck. His first reaction is to scream his conviction of her palpable infidelity at her, and he refuses to be persuaded by her usual half-hearted evasions:

' ... no doubt remained any longer in Emilio's mind that she had just come from the arms of another, and there rushed into his mind – as the only means of saving himself from all this filth – a plan of superhuman energy. He must not go to bed with her; he must drive her away on the spot and never, never see her again. But he had already experienced the meaning of "never again": one long agony, one continual regret, hours of endless agitation, hours of tormented dreams followed by hopeless languor, then a void, the death of imagination and desire, a state more painful than any other. He was afraid. He drew her to him and avenged himself solely by saying: "I am not worth much more than you are" ... '

It is a compelling, deeply understood, depiction of the psychology of sexual self-abasement. Nevertheless Emilio's humiliation walks alongside a kind of glory. His queen of the slums in the Austro-Hungarian empire's premier port city cannot express her pride in her sexuality as eloquently as Shakespeare's Cleopatra does in her indignant speech to the departing Antony: 'none our parts so poor,/ But was a race of heaven'. Yet in this moment Angiolina has her own dignity, expressed in the unvarnished terms she is accustomed to articulate. ' ... it was her turn to rebel now, and struggling out of his arms she said emphatically: "I have never allowed anyone to treat me like this. I am going."'

We like her the better for her sense of her own worth. As for Emilio: 'when he saw her so full of determination he could not help admiring her, shaken as he was by the mere idea of making such a resolution'.

Nothing, in fact, that Emilio does diminishes Angiolina. As his own moral disintegration progresses she stays splendidly outside the process. A phase of morbid insistence on her assuming the role of sick nurse in the event of his falling ill, draws from her the splendidly prosaic reaction "'Oh, it would be lovely."' When he develops a fantastical socialistic theory to explain their 'unhappiness' based on an exaggerated attitude to her poverty, she remains magnificently indifferent to his intentions for those of her class: "'If everything was to be divided there wouldn't be much left for anyone. The working classes are jealous good-for-nothings and will never succeed however much you do for them."'

The final disintegration of their relationship, in a welter of lies from Angiolina and an episode of quite shocking naked violence on his part is a thing of effortless vividness from Svevo. It bears the stamp of what F.R. Leavis, in a completely different context, called 'the weight of felt experience'. We are back outside in the windswept cold and dark of a Trieste night with Ettore Schmitz, shaking with uncontrollable anger at the mere thought of the infidelities his mistress Giuseppina Zergol enacts within.

Emilio hurls demented abuse at Angiolina even while he cannot bear to be parted from her physical presence. ' ... the effort to hold her fast had become an all-absorbing motive to Emilio; he dug his fingers voluptuously into her soft flesh'. When she eventually breaks from him and flees into the darkness, the nadir of baseness to which he has descended is symbolized by the utter futility of his next action. 'He never even attempted to catch her up; he stooped down and looked for a stone, but when he could not find one he collected some small pebbles which he hurled after her. The wind carried them along and one must have struck her for she uttered a cry of terror. The others struck the dry branches of the trees and produced a sound which was ridiculously out of proportion to the anger which had raised his arm to throw them.' The episode is given the greater poignancy from his having abandoned to others his watch at the bedside of his dying sister at home to make this assignation with Angiolina.

The deathbed scenes which remove Amalia from the story have divided critics. For Furbank they are 'what a dozen other novelists have done as well' – which does not of course necessarily mean that they are bad writing. Moloney, I think rightly, compares the effect they make on us with the deathbed of Nitti's mother in *Una vita* – which is one of the best things in that novel. They bring out the best in Balli, even if his 'love' for Amalia that consoles her last hours has a strongly aesthetic dimension. The jealousy of a fancied rival for his affections, which bursts from her almost in the last moments of her life, and his futile attempt to assure her of his 'fidelity' are strangely moving. Her death rattle, described by Svevo as 'the lament of matter which, already abandoned by the spirit and beginning to disintegrate, was uttering the sounds it had learned during its long period of painful consciousness' is a powerfully bleak summary of her existence. Svevo has laughed at many things and many people in *Senilità*. He is not laughing here.

What are we to make of Angiolina's 'fate' in the novel? Needless to say Sorniani is the instrument of communicating the news of it to Emilio. She has run off with a crooked bank cashier who has defrauded his own establishment. It's a perfunctory treatment of the episode, reported in a throw-away single sentence, with none of that revelling in circumstances and psychology that normally accompanies Sorniani's revelations to Emilio.

Is this merely a case of convenience for Svevo? A hasty, barely-disguised conversion of the facts of his own affair to fictional purposes? (After leaving him Zergol had run off to join a circus as a bareback rider.) Or is it a Naturalistic fate for the 'whore' character, analogous, say, to that of Zola's Nana? A form of impartial punishment – though it does not go by such a name – for her destructive tendencies? In any event it's a defeat for her for which we feel slightly sad. We had hoped somehow that she would remain just ahead of the game. She is not a wicked woman. She gives freely of herself. She has actually given more to Emilio, in terms of an erotic life vividly experienced, than he would otherwise have known.

To do him justice he does not deny this, although his memory of her becomes bound in a fantasy that has little to do with the earthy realities of the experience. 'Angiolina underwent a strange metamorphosis in the writer's idle imagination. She preserved all her own beauty, but acquired as well all the qualities of Amalia ... She grew sad and dispirited, her eye acquired an intellectual clarity. He saw her before him as on an altar, the personification of thought and suffering, and he never ceased loving her ... '

The ending of the novel was greatly admired by Joyce who had its final paragraphs by heart. Angiolina has become a woman who in Emilio's memory 'thinks and sometimes cries, thinks as though the secret of the universe had been explained to her or the secret of her own existence, and is sad as though in the whole wide world she could not find one single solitary *deo gratias*'.

This is not convincing, after all that has gone before it, and its endorsement by the normally sceptical Joyce, in this instance seduced by its – actually superficial – poetry, cannot make it so. It is impossible to imagine that it is an ending that harnesses Svevo's true convictions at the end of a novel that is not only a marvelous anatomy of a powerful, if totally misdirected, erotic passion but also a powerful social document.

It is not thus that Angiolina lives on, if we care to try to imagine her life beyond the novel.

On the book's penultimate page her reincarnation and successor, in the form of her little sister, is ready and willing to do what has to be done to fill her absence. Since Angiolina fled from her home the girl has developed a 'pretty curtsey' and a mature handshake for male visitors. When her mother cannot face Emilio, who has come to enquire of news about her sister, she takes it on herself to give him a most adult welcome, apologizing for her mother's behaviour with the fiction that she is not well and inviting him to come back another day.

As we have already seen, her reaction to an incautious avuncular kiss on the forehead from Emilio is to fling her arms round his neck and cover his face with 'kisses that were by no means childish'.

Emilio's disgust at the deployment of these desperate survival tactics from the girl is of a piece with his blindness over most aspects of the imperatives propelling Angiolina, and all women in her circumstances. The older sister lives before us again in this ragamuffin of a younger sibling who will do all she can to ensure her survival, and that of her family. It is an imperative that is beyond the perception of a man as deluded as Emilio has become.

5

Enter Zeno Cosini

PUBLISHED IN 1923, *LA COSCIENZA DI ZENO* was first translated into English as *The Confessions of Zeno* by Beryl de Zoete and published in America in 1930. The translation eventually took its place among the five volumes of Secker & Warburg's Uniform Edition of Svevo's works in English (1962-69). It was the translation through which generations of readers in Britain knew it through the Penguin paperback from the mid-1960s onwards.

Confessions of Zeno was the title by which Svevo's novel was known in the English-speaking world until 2001 when a new translation by William Weaver appeared as *Zeno's Conscience*. First published in America, this translation, with its new title, has since been adopted by Penguin.

This is a pity. One meaning of the Italian word *coscienza* is indeed 'conscience'. But since this is the very last moral attribute we could possibly ascribe to the book's shameless protagonist, such a title does not at all convey Svevo's intentions. In his translator's introduction Weaver goes to some lengths to explain to us his reasons for the change. He tells us that to one of his Roman Catholic background the original choice of 'confessions' in the title was 'misleading, placing Zeno Cosini in a line descended from Augustine and Rousseau ... it had a religious, sacramental connotation that I felt was unsuitable'. What on earth the thoughts and doings of such a thorough-going agnostic Jew as Zeno Cosini have to do with Mr Weaver's precious Roman Catholic scruples is difficult to imagine.

Weaver was well aware that *coscienza* can also signify 'consciousness' or 'knowledge'. But clearly 'The Consciousness of Zeno' would have made a ponderous title. Unfortunately for us, at this point in his deliberations an article in the *Times Literary Supplement* came to his rescue: 'I read that in the past, the English word "conscience" had also had the meaning of "consciousness"', Weaver tells us. *TLS* directed him to *Hamlet* 3.1.83: 'Thus conscience does make cowards of us all.' In fact scholars are still undecided on whether Shakespeare here meant 'conscience' as we know it – the inner voice of moral judgment – or 'consciousness'. It seems to me inescapable that the former is intended. No one reading or hearing Hamlet's speech today would dream it might mean anything else. But this is all by the way. The 17th-century meaning Weaver wants to impose on the word 'conscience' simply no longer exists in the language. Its use today signifies exclusively the sort of guilt feelings of which Zeno Cosini is entirely free.

It seems a crying shame that misguided religious scruples have been allowed to banish the original English title which is ironical, vital and absolutely appropriate to what is mischievously presented by the author as revelations from the psychiatrist's couch – for one that is inert and misleading. Svevo certainly would not have understood it. We are now all the prisoners of Mr Weaver's conscience. Perhaps a man of his solemnity and self-importance was not the man to be let loose by his editors on choosing an English title for this novel.

As for the relative merits of the de Zoete and Weaver translations, it is actually remarkable how modern de Zoete's effort continues to feel after 80 years. But its modernity is not its decisive virtue. For me, she is consistently much closer in outlook, than Weaver is, to the utterly agnostic texture of Zeno's mind.

For Svevo *La coscienza di Zeno* marks the breakthrough in content, form and style that cuts him asunder from his previous writing efforts and announces him as a modernist and one of the great comic novelists of the 20th century. It is almost as if he had suddenly cast off mental shackles, and liberated himself from stumbling around in the wretched milieux of his previous protagonists Alfonso Nitti and Emilio Brentani. Whereas in both *La vita* and *Senilità* he never seemed to be able satisfactorily to construct and control a mechanism for using and analyzing his insights, and his rich exposure to the ethos of his home city, here he is suddenly a master of his universe.

Most important, realism is jettisoned. Though his protagonist Zeno is, as surely as Nitti and Brentani were, apparently trapped in a web of neurotic self-analysis, he is really its master. In *La vita* and *Senilità* it was a case of protagonist vs the universe; in *La coscienza* the world *is* Zeno's.

In spite of all his confusions, misunderstandings and defeats, he ends up bestriding it, not unlike his creator, the man who had previously stumbled into the calling of warship paint manufacture and made himself the principal exponent of the business.

Has Svevo jettisoned sentiment and tenderness in leaving this creative past behind him? Yes. Does it matter? No. This is a picaresque novel, and Zeno is the *picaro* par excellence, a man whose mental plots bamboozle those around him no less than they frequently confuse himself. He would have been quite at home in the pages of *Don Quixote*.

Zeno Cosini is quintessentially the 'unreliable narrator'. We are alerted to the fact in a 'preface' from Dr S, his analyst. Neither of Svevo's previous protagonists of course were particularly strong on self knowledge, or a perception of what constituted the truth of affairs in the world outside them. But they tried to be. Zeno does not. Like Sir Thomas Browne's 'man, that great and true Amphibium' he is at ease in the universe and has no difficulty in living in 'divided and distinguished worlds'.

The subject of his third chapter (which is located in the book after a brief preface and introduction), smoking and the difficulty of giving it up, leads us immediately to what we must expect from him in this regard. Every day for Zeno will be the day of the last cigarette. I can't help feeling that the title de Zoete gives this chapter, in Italian *Il fumo*, which she translates as 'The Last Cigarette' establishes much more effectively than Weaver's literal 'Smoke' what is to become a refrain throughout the novel – as it was in Svevo's life. *Il fumo* clearly refers to cigarette smoking here. It might just, I suppose, refer to the smokescreen with which Zeno will constantly attempt to obscure our perception, as well as those of his fellow characters in the book, but I think not. As if a Zeno would open his account with us by owning up to such a thing! We have to be made to believe in the power of the mythical 'last cigarette' as much as he wants to – as much as his creator did almost to the last moments of his life.

The fundamental difference between Zeno and his predecessor protagonists is his unabashed cheerfulness. Unlike Nitti and Brentani he reinvents his universe every day he wakes, and clothes himself afresh in his entirely individualistic vision of the world.

As a man in search of a wife he woos the young and beautiful Ada, daughter of the Malfenti family. Moving swiftly on from her when he realizes that Ada is spoken for by the young and handsome Guido, a man he detests as having talents he notably lacks, he almost immediately proposes to her sister Alberta. When she rejects him very maturely and pleasantly, for one so young, he is, within half a page of the novel, applying to Augusta, the eldest and plainest of the Malfenti sisters. It is, as he admits, 'a very rough and ready proposal'. But she is wise enough to accept it – and not only for her own satisfaction as the family Plain Jane who may never do any better. She can see that Zeno needs someone like her to make something of himself. And she is right. Marrying her is the best thing he has done in his life to that point.

Beginning the story of his association with the Malfenti family as a weak and ineffectual character in the mould of Nitti and Brentani, Zeno ends up turning the tables on the seemingly 'strong' and 'successful' Guido, to become not only a successful businessman but to bask at last in the admiration, if not love, of his continually desired sister-in-law Ada. While it is clear that she is not going to indulge him or herself in any infraction of family harmony by having an affair with him, she does give him the pleasure of hearing himself called, 'the best man in our family'. It's something of a reward for his quite-accidently virtuous behaviour towards her.

Even Zeno's conduct of his extra-marital affairs is, accidentally, a triumph. While the handsome, narcissistic Guido will, once married, carelessly rub his wife's nose in his sexual escapade with his young secretary and earn her contempt, Zeno not only escapes detection in his amour with a young singer, but from it manages (quite inadvertently) to align himself psychologically with his affair in such a way that it increases his sense of his wife's merits and ends up in his loving her the more. In the end it is Guido who becomes (even if accidentally) the suicide after going bankrupt. And the beautiful Ada, shorn of her looks after contracting a particularly cruel form of goitre, survives to reflect on what might have been, as she prepares to leave Trieste to live with her in-laws' family in Argentina.

In 'The Last Cigarette' we encounter Zeno, in mature age reviewing, from almost his first memories of his conduct, the extent of his mendacity to himself. This is measured in the prodigious list of 'last cigarettes' whose ashes litter his progress through life. He tells us 'I find the following entry on the front page of a dictionary, beautifully written and adorned with a good many flourishes: *2 February, 1886. Today I finish my law studies and take up chemistry. Last cigarette!!*'

Such notifications are to punctuate the record of his progress through studies and the other methods he adopts as he attempts to alight on a modus vivendi that might save him from sheer idleness. Chemistry, needless to say, does not suit. ' ... when I could no longer accept all the endless combinations of carbonic acid gas I went back to law. That was a mistake, alas, and that too had to be celebrated by a last cigarette.' The rising tide of addiction is his constant companion. 'Once when I was a student I changed my lodgings, and had to have the walls of my room repapered at my own expense. Probably I left that room just because it had become the tomb of my good resolutions, and I felt it had become impossible to form any such resolutions there.'

Among the ruins of his resolve he accepts a suggestion from his wife that he enter a sanatorium in an attempt to rid himself of his habit. Here, on his first night under strict conditions which amount (to his wife's amusement) almost to incarceration, 'I took out my last cigarette but one, and began smoking it greedily. I explained to the doctor that I had only brought two and that I was going to stop smoking on the stroke of midnight.'

Almost immediately his resolution is subverted by paranoia, triggered by his sudden conviction of an attraction between his wife and the handsome young doctor in charge of the sanatorium, as they leave him with his 'jailer', Giovanna, a woman of indeterminate age. 'Suddenly I realized that I had smoked my last cigarette and it was not yet midnight but eleven o'clock, an impossible hour for a last cigarette'.

In a panic of jealousy he calls for Giovanna and tries to bribe her to get him a cigarette. What ensues gives an interesting insight into the character of Zeno, and explains a good deal about his own kind of 'success' with women in the novel, which is not necessarily a sexual one, but a quality of ease in the presence of the female psyche that enables women to trust, and make confidences in, him. Over a bottle of brandy – permitted under the easy sanatorium regime while (for him) cigarettes are not – Giovanna begins telling him about her married life.

The episode is not central to the novel but it alerts us to a good deal of what constitutes Zeno's psychological type, where women are concerned. Giovanna is one of those minor characters who occur momentarily in the pages of *La coscienza*. By the time we are well into the three chapters, 'The Story of My Marriage'; 'Wife and Mistress' and 'A Business Partnership', which make up the novel's heart, we will probably have forgotten her – on a first reading at any rate.

Yet here, in a very short acquaintance she becomes vividly and recognizably real, a woman who ploughs resolutely through the morass of her life, negotiating its difficulties without complaint, a sort of Mother Courage in minor mode. Although of the bourgeoisie, Zeno is not a snob, and he gets on well with people in all walks of life. Unlike most men, he is not, in spite of his now twin obsessions (smoking and jealousy of his wife), one to inflict a conversation based on the preoccupations of his own life on a woman. 'I begged Giovanna to entertain me a little, and when she said that she couldn't think of anything that would interest me I asked her to tell me about her family, adding that almost everyone living had at least one.' The invitation is to lead to confidences of the kind that, as it happens, particularly interest him. It is almost as if his own crooked thought processes draw out this stranger's hitherto unutterable secrets, which include the kind of inadvertently devious behaviour to which he is himself prone.

'Then Giovanna grew thoughtful and asked me if I thought the dead could see what the living were doing. Yes, I thought so. But then she wanted to know whether, when people were dead, they would discover everything that had happened while they were alive. For a moment this question actually succeeded in distracting me from my own troubles. It was pronounced in a very soft voice as if Giovanna had purposely lowered it so that the dead should not hear it.'

Zeno gently elicits the tale of her life from her. This apparently simple woman's story becomes, in Svevo's hands, a somewhat Zeno-esque affair itself: it includes her almost immediate unfaithfulness to her now-dead husband; and a pregnancy from that affair which luckily the fact of her marriage absorbed without its being noticed.

'Moved by a certain brotherly sympathy I tried to diminish her grief by saying that I thought the dead probably did know everything, but that there were certain things they would not bother their heads about.'

Giovanna, packed off to bed with the remains of the bottle of brandy, having also been persuaded to furnish a packet of cigarettes to her patient, is not likely to oppose the now immediate termination of his 'treatment' on which Zeno is determined. Very soon he is in the street, and soon afterwards on his own doorstep. His accusatory remark to his wife who is not at all surprised at his return: "'I believe you have taken advantage of my absence to change the position of that chest of drawers'", is a classic example of the

Freudian displacement reaction and, as we shall learn, one of Zeno's most prominent characteristics. In reality ' ... at that moment I was hunting in every corner to see if I could find a trace of the elegant little body of Dr Muli'.

Giovanna does not reappear in Zeno's life. But her brief appearance in it tells us a good deal about his tangential relationship with reality.

When the question of matrimony begins to touch him, Zeno is, needless to say, an unorthodox wooer. As he freely admits to us, he comes to a wife through admiration of the man who will become his father-in-law, a successful business man and vulgarian whose character is at a polar remove from his own. On Zeno's admission, his own ideas of business are somewhat quixotic ' ... if I see that a tax has been reduced my thoughts turn immediately to Cobden and Liberalism. This seems so uplifting an idea that I have no room left for my own particular merchandise'.

Giovanni Malfenti is by contrast 'ignorant and pushing. But his ignorance gave one the impression of quiet strength which fascinated me ... The few ideas that he kept in his head had been weighed, analyzed and sifted by him with such care and lucidity ... that they seemed to have become part of him like his limbs ... I was lacking ideas like that and I clung to him in the hope of enriching myself'.

In the event, typically, Zeno's sole piece of business success under Malfenti's tutelage comes from forgetting to take his advice to sell some shares on a falling market. Malfenti sells his, the shares then rise, and for a few days Zeno is able to bask in the unmerited aura of having a shrewd business nose.

Zeno's choice of a mate from among such a man's four daughters is, like his business dealings, an utterly haphazard affair. Circumstances, not his own will, dictate the outcome. He, however, conceives of his task as being simplicity itself. The eldest, Augusta, is too plain. Anna is a child of seven. Of the two prettiest Alberta is still at school, while Ada, a true beauty, is in the flush of young womanhood. 'And so I set out to win Ada, and persisted in trying to make her laugh at me, forgetting that what I had first chosen her for was her seriousness. I am rather fantastic I know, but to her I must have seemed positively unbalanced.'

Zeno proceeds to pave the pathway, which he hopes will lead to his acceptance by Ada with obstacles entirely of his own making. His gaffes reveal the essential Zeno whom Ada may not like – but whom we find irresistible. 'I liked her simple way of talking the more because I myself could not open my mouth without misrepresenting things or people, for otherwise I should have seen no use in talking at all. Talking itself seemed to me an event in itself which must not be hampered by any other events.' Zeno, in short, cannot help reinventing the universe as it takes his fancy – even when conscious that the components that inhabit it may be downright falsehoods, even as he is describing them.

His wooing of Ada misfires at every turn. His tale of the Angora cat asleep on the counter of a London bookshop which scratches him, and thereby confirms his hatred of all things English, amuses the Malfenti sisters and their mother – but falls flat with Ada, whose logical mind demands a human agency to account for this sudden prejudice against a whole nation.

His attempt to ingratiate himself with Ada's favourite aunt is equally ill starred. Having been told that this aunt normally suffers from a 'bilious complexion' he is convinced that he has found a way to a handsome compliment. 'I had found what I wanted. Looking affectionately into the old woman's face I said: "You are looking much better madam."' This causes immediate affront. Signora Malfenti (one of those mothers whom a putative wooer of her daughter always gets on better with than he does with the object of his desire) is forced to come to a good-natured rescue.

'"But you don't mean to suggest that Aunt Rosina has got fatter?" The devil! So that was what had made the old lady so angry. She was almost as big as her brother but was still hoping to get thin.'

After this catalogue of social disasters Zeno concludes that the game is up. He will break with the family completely. Only a Zeno could think that his plan will be even intelligible to those it is directed at, let alone likely to be effective. 'I hit on what seemed to me a discreet and pleasant, if slightly ironical way of confirming my purpose. I hastened to a florist and selected a magnificent bouquet of flowers, which I addressed to Signora Malfenti, accompanied by my visiting card, on which nothing was written except the date, which I should never forget and which probably Ada and her mother would never forget either. May the fifth, the anniversary of Napoleon's death.'

We do not learn what the reception of this gesture is. It is to be assumed that the ironic minutiae of its symbolism, so telling to Zeno in his hour of fantastic resolve, are not perceived by his hostess. Yet it's one that gives him undoubted pleasure, creating a mini-universe replete with meanings and echoes that connect him and his desires to the great currents of history. That this self-delusion is to be scattered to the winds within the next twenty-four hours does not matter in the slightest.

Zeno's paints his 'love' for Ada in most vivid colours, backed up by an apparently rational analysis: 'I not only wanted to possess her, I wanted her for my wife, with her cold face and angular body, and her serious nature which could not and never would appreciate my humour; I would give it all up for her, and she would inspire me to live an intelligent and industrious life. I wanted the whole of her, I expected everything from her.' These fantastic notions are soon to receive their fatal check.

In a flash of insight he realizes that his putative in-laws do not want him to marry Ada – and nor does she. He will actually marry the right woman and she the wrong man. Undoubtedly he and Ada would never have been happy together, while Augusta is the only woman in the novel who could have kept him on the rails. But this has no bearing on his continuing to be 'in love' with Ada, almost the only person in his life as we see it in *La coscienza*, with whom he keeps some kind of faith.

Zeno has vividly imagined a rival in his love for Ada some time before her future husband, Guido Speier, actually makes an entrance. 'Every time I met a well-dressed, healthy-looking man who appeared to be at peace with himself and the world, I hated him because I thought he would do for Ada. The chief thing I remember about those days is the jealousy that settled like a black cloud on my life.'

While wandering the streets, waiting for the blow to fall, he discovers the hypochondria which, with its concomitant capacity to conjure up timely psychosomatic complaints, is to prove a valuable crutch to this, the healthiest and toughest of men, in situations of psychological discomposure. The catalyst is a meeting in a café with an old schoolfriend, Tullio, now crippled with rheumatism. The man's account of an exhaustive regimen of cures, diets and physical therapy for atrophied muscles points the way to a similar escape from reality to a fellow hypochondriac in the making. As Zeno listens to Tullio's enumeration of the fifty-four muscle movements that apparently accompany each half second of human ambulation, Zeno suddenly has a displacement reaction to hand for those moments of stress that litter his own life. 'I listened in bewilderment. I at once directed my attention to my legs and tried to discover the infernal machine. I thought I had succeeded in finding it. I could not of course distinguish all its fifty-four parts, but I discovered something terrifically complicated which seemed to get out of order directly I began thinking about it. I limped as I left the café ... '

Zeno has discovered a companion for life. But this companion does not become a tyrant. It is something that can be summoned at convenience. There is nothing neurasthenic about Zeno. He is no *malade imaginaire*. As D.J. Enright put it in an *Encounter* review of 1962: 'A real *malade imaginaire* is deceiving himself, whereas Zeno is an imaginary *malade imaginaire*. The play of the *Confessions* is between self-deception, engaging attempts at deceiving the reader, and truth telling.'

The materialization of Guido, just as Zeno thinks he has Ada all to himself on a quiet walk after mass, brings out the splendid worst – or best, depending on one's viewpoint – in Zeno. He is about to declare himself to Ada, characteristically puzzling out a formulation of words with which to do so and failing to come to the point, when she is hailed from behind by a fresh young man's voice. 'I turned indignantly. Who had dared to interrupt the explanations I had not even begun?'

Gallingly, he observes the light that comes into Ada's face and eyes, as she turns and welcomes 'Signor Guido'. To her he is always more formally, less intimately 'Signor Cosini'. He is conscious of the rictus of a smile he is compelled to summon up to match Ada's spontaneous one as she introduces them.

'His name was Guido Speier. My smile became more spontaneous because I at once saw an opportunity to say something disagreeable to him.' His insulting assumption, immediately voiced, that Guido must be German is politely corrected by the young man, who not only disabuses him but rubs salt in the wound by proceeding to discourse in fluent Tuscan, whereas Zeno and Ada are restricted to their telltale Triestine dialect.

Zeno's recently acquired displacement tic now kicks in. But his companions, happy in their youth and their instinctive attraction to each other, do not notice his limp. Hoping against hope, the infatuated Zeno tries to keep his nerve and hold his ground. 'Ada was walking between us, and her face wore a vague unchanging expression of happiness which was almost a smile. That happy look was new to her. For whom was the smile intended? Might it not be for me, whom she had not seen for so long?'

Every step is destined to be a torment. A shared interest, struck up between the two young folk, in spiritualism and table turning, dismissed by Zeno as bunkum, only makes him more determined than ever to win the day against his rival. But his irritation against Ada's gullibility on this topic conspires only to make him rude and even less attractive to her.

Salt is rubbed into his emotional wounds when he subsequently encounters Giovanni Malfenti who assures him that at their house that evening he will hear 'a violinist such as one does not often hear'. It is of course to be Guido, whose proficiency will present a fresh threat to Zeno, who has for years struggled to attain a bare competence on the instrument.

When Zeno arrives at the Malfenti's he finds a table turning session in progress, presided over by Guido, with Ada as his gullible amanuensis. What follows is quintessential Zeno, one of the book's most hilarious episodes. As Guido, self-appointed 'chairman' of this farrago of nonsense, disposes its participants about the room for a table-turning session with the aim of summoning the spirits of the dead, Zeno exultantly finds himself not merely sitting next to, but crushed up against, Ada in the darkness.

Interestingly, his (as it happens, imagined) contact with the girl is one of the few really sexually sensuous passages in a book which in general takes the physical component of traffic between the sexes rather for granted. Sex, in the sense in which we see it in action in *Una vita* and *Senilità* is largely a matter-of-fact business in *La coscienza*. But Zeno's unconsummated relationship with Ada has something of the sense of anticipation of that of Emilio for Angiolina.

'I had reproached myself so often for allowing things to reach this point, without having had any explanation with Ada, that now I had her next to me, and in the dark too, I was only restrained by the delicious sense of having her so close after I had feared to lose her forever. I preferred to breathe the fragrance of the soft texture of her dress which was touching me, and I thought that, close as we were together, my feet must be actually touching hers.'

As Guido continues to issue his instructions to the company, as to the most likely way to invoke the spirits, Zeno has one of his moments of absolute decision.

'I was glad that he was still busying himself about the table. It was clear now that Ada had resigned herself to bearing almost the whole of my weight! She must love me or she would not have stood it. At last the hour of explanation had arrived. I removed my arm from the table and put it gently round her waist.

'"I love you, Ada!" I said in a low voice, putting my face close to hers so that she could hear better.

'The girl did not reply at once. Then she murmured in a faint voice – but Augusta's:

'"Why have you not been here for so long?"'

In the midst of this crushing defeat of his hopes Zeno does actually manage to behave rather well to the young woman he has inadvertently so cruelly humiliated. For once, common sense, not usually a guiding feature in his dealings with women he desires, comes to his rescue. 'I obeyed my first instinct not to answer her

question, but after a moment's hesitation I said to her: "I am glad I
have confided in you, Augusta, for I know how kind you are."'

This is the first of three more declarations of love Zeno is to
make that evening: the second, to the real Ada, the third to Alberta
and the fourth, this time intentionally, to Augusta.

In the meantime Zeno finds in the situation a momentary
diversion from his mission to further his cause among the Malfenti
girls. At this juncture Guido's admonition to him – and by
association Augusta – for breaking silence in detriment to the
important business of raising the spirits is the perfect opportunity
for a revenge that will render his rival absurd. With a little tweaking
of the table-turning ritual he is able to convince the gullible Guido
that he has made contact with a deceased Speier grandfather, who
is, conveniently, to be made the harbinger of bad news. It's childish,
of course, especially in one of his age, but, as so often in such
instances in the book, we are utterly on the side of Zeno.

The solemnity of Guido's conversation with this supposed
ancestor is too idiotic for words. Yet, as Zeno is to learn, in the
country of the blind the one-eyed man is not necessarily king. When
it at last becomes evident to Guido that terrestrial muscle and not
spiritual power is behind the table's reply to his queries, Zeno's
good-natured confession, 'I was tired of waiting for the spirits, and
amused myself by taking their place', does him no good with the
besotted Ada, who angrily turns her back on him. Nevertheless, he
is not to be deflected from his intention, inoculated by the strength
of his conviction of their joint destiny against the improbability of
success. 'I was oppressed by the fact that Ada was compromising
herself so dreadfully. It caused me as much pain as to hear that my
mistress had been unfaithful to me. In spite of the affection she
showed to Guido I thought she might still be mine ...'

When Giovanni asks Guido to display his powers on the violin the scene is set for an even more resounding, and this time public, defeat for Zeno. Although he has admitted that he 'was hypocritical enough to join Giovanni in begging Guido to play for us', he is now exposed to a performance which, as he well knows, is superior to anything he himself could achieve. Guido's bow has no sooner touched the strings than ' ... the great Bach appeared in person. Never before or since have I felt so intensely the beauty of that music, which seemed to have grown out of the four strings like a Michelangelo angel out of a block of marble.' The piece is Bach's great Chaconne. If for nothing else we give Zeno full marks for his insight as a music critic. But his jealous admiration is at war with his desire to find fault. 'I tried to escape from the music, saying to myself: "To play like this you only need a great sense of rhythm, a sure hand, and a capacity for imitation. I have none of these things, which is not a sign of inferiority, but merely my misfortune."'

When Guido finishes, with even a lay audience recognizing that they have heard a marvel, Zeno hypocritically leads the congratulations, but with the cavilling reservation '" ... but I don't understand why toward the end you played those notes staccato, though Bach has marked them legato ... Bach," I added, "uses such humble means to attain his end that an artificial bowing like that is quite out of place."' Guido is not to be abashed. This is his hour. Golden youth can get away with anything at this moment. '"Perhaps Bach wasn't familiar with that means of giving expression. I make him a present of it!"' Right or wrong, we are wholeheartedly in sympathy with Zeno as he faces the united hostility of the entire room in lonely indignation: 'He dared to put himself above Bach, and no one protested; whereas they laughed at me, who had merely ventured to put myself above Guido.'

There is no time to digest the implication of all this in terms of his determination to press on in his wooing of Ada. Events now propel him into it.

A scream from the child Anna in an adjacent room suddenly virtually empties the drawing room, leaving Zeno alone with Ada who has been left clutching the precious violin, which Guido has thrust into her hands at this moment of domestic emergency. For once Zeno gives himself no time to procrastinate. Since she seems happy not to follow the others in the succouring of the child, he pops the question: 'I tried to be as simple and brief as possible. I was also compelled to be, for I could hardly breathe. I said "I love you, Ada, may I speak to your father?"'

The response is everything he had not hoped for. 'She sat staring at me in horror and amazement. I was afraid she was going to begin screaming too, like her little sister'. To compound his blunder, not waiting for a response, he now encumbers himself with all the diversionary clutter that is his hallmark when trying to develop what he thinks is rational explanation. His assurance to her that she cannot possibly be surprised, cannot possibly be thinking he is in fact in love with Augusta, only infuriates her further on behalf of her sister. After what comes perilously close to developing into an unseemly brawl, she collects herself to give him an answer: '"As for me ... I wonder that such a thing entered your head."'

Rebuffed in these most decisive terms, he is about to leave the house, but is left not only with a certain feeling of mission unaccomplished, but with the certainty that his failure with Ada will undoubtedly give him a sleepless night of ratiocination. A bad night's sleep is something the valetudinarian cannot abide. Any and everything thing must be done to avoid it. When the party regroups in the drawing room after the interruption, he finds himself seated by Alberta. Suddenly one of his father's maxims floats appositely into his mind: '"Choose a young wife, it will be easier for you to educate her to suit you."' It's the sort of pedestrian counsel, coming from a man as unlike Zeno as his father was, that would not normally form part of Zeno's vocabulary for living. But it's convenient to the situation. He allows himself a moment as the *homme moyen sensuel*: 'This decided me. I again looked at Alberta. I undressed her in imagination and the soft young body I pictured delighted me. I said: "Listen Alberta! I've got an idea. Has it ever occurred to you that you are old enough to get married?"'

Alberta's negative is actually a much more collected affair than her elder sister's was. Her sole ambition, she tells him, is to become a writer and she has no intention of marrying at present. It is certainly a more mature response than the reaction to it of her one-minute wonder of a suitor whose pique leads him to the hilariously huffy response: '"I shall now propose to Augusta, and tell everyone I married her because both her sisters refused me!" I laughed with extravagant good humour as I reflected on the strangeness of my proposal.'

The object of this chameleon passion is luckily at hand in the passage – Augusta is carrying a medicinal drink on a tray for the afflicted child. 'I ran after her calling her by name, and she leaned against a wall and waited for me. I stood facing her, and said without a moment's hesitation: "Listen to me Augusta! Would you like us to get married?"' Although it is, as he readily admits, 'a very rough and ready proposal', he is at least as good as his word to Alberta and explains that he has already proposed to, and been refused by, Ada and her.

We have to admire Augusta here. It is Svevo's genius that in spite of everything she never appears as the put-upon Plain Jane, accepted on sufferance. Her reply, delivered without pique, '"So you want me to understand and always to remember that you don't love me?"' is worthy of Zeno himself. He is thrown into a mental spin by it. 'What did she mean by that sibylline saying? Was it the prelude to consent? Did she mean that she would remember during all the years she would have to live with me? I felt like someone who has put himself in a dangerous position on purpose to kill himself, and then has to strain every nerve in order to save his own life.'

When she admirably puts an end to his mental seesawing with a candid declaration of her (and his) situation, '"You need a woman, Zeno, to live with you and look after you. I will be that woman"', he is overcome with a feeling of relief. 'At last I had obtained certainty'.

Characteristically, more important for the valetudinarian, at the end of a dinner which becomes an emotional family affair replete with an exhausting parade of congratulations to the newly engaged couple: 'I felt terribly sleepy, which was a proof that I had acted with a certain amount of foresight. I was going to get a good night at last.' Among literature's litany of strange reasons for making a proposal of marriage Zeno's must be the only one based on the assurance of its securing a night's sound sleep.

For Zeno, of course, marriage is not the end of the story, but merely the beginning of the most creative (in terms of his unique psychological proclivities) phase of his life. He has already shared with us a secret that he cannot share with his wife-to-be. 'It was on the tip of my tongue to say that it was because I could not bear the thought of never meeting Ada again that I was willing even to become her brother-in-law.' Such a resolution of circumstances is not just a commonplace declaration of lust for Ada which he fancies that he might translate at some point into an affair with her, but is, rather, characteristic of a circuitous approach to life whose ends can simply never be imagined from its aims, either by himself, or us.

The drawback is that on this night, the restorative sleep to which

Zeno has been looking forward all evening is to be delayed. Guido foists his company on him, as he walks home, drink, so we suppose, having increased a propensity for a friendly inquisition into Zeno's journey towards his engagement. This nosiness immediately brings on the psychosomatic limp. 'I found Guido's company almost intolerable. He enquired with great curiosity into the story of my love for Augusta ... I told him brazenly that I had fallen in love with her at first sight ... The pain I was suffering made me talkative, as if I were trying to shout it down. But I talked too much, and if Guido had really been listening he would have discovered that I was not so much in love with Augusta as all that.'

In the event Guido is only concerned with airing his own view of the Malfenti family. It comes as no surprise to us that in spite of his popularity with young women he is a misogynist. As he expounds his notions on this topic it becomes evident that his ideas are straight from the unsavoury pages of Otto Weininger's *Sex and Character* (1903), a book in which the Jewish anti-semitic philosopher (who shot himself in the year of its publication) writes extensively of similarities he detects between women and the Jewish race, harping on what he regards as the weakness, instability and despicable nature of both.

When this offensive exposition begins to embrace even Ada herself, Zeno is suddenly struck by the idea that the object of his love can actually hear Guido's insults, and is seized by the fantastic notion that he might kill him. By now, the pair have climbed up the steep Via Belvedere. Ada's suitor, exhausted by the vehemence of his diatribe, has lain down to rest on a low wall directly overhanging the street running thirty-odd feet below them. 'He was lying with his arms folded behind his head, and it would only need a sudden good push to throw him completely off his balance.'

Guido owes his salvation at this time to his companion's deeply-rooted valetudinarianism which provides a farcical antidote to his resolve. 'I had got engaged to Augusta in order to have a good night. How should I be able to sleep if I killed Guido? This thought saved both of us ... ' It's a quintessentially Zeno-esque reason for *not* killing someone.

It is certainly not going to come as any surprise to us that on Zeno's wedding day it is the groom, not the bride, who is late for the ceremony. Reasons for prevaricating/procrastinating/cancelling come tumbling from his mind in a torrent of ironies that sum up what we have seen of Zeno's character to this point – his instinctive resort to alternative strategies for coping with what faces him that will after all get him to the desired goal, if by unforeseen routes.

'I was supposed to be with Augusta by eight o'clock in the morning, but at a quarter to eight I was still in bed, smoking furiously ... The absurdity of my marriage became evident, now that I no longer wanted to remain close to Ada ... Besides: Augusta had been a charming fiancée, but one could never know how she would behave directly she was married ... Fortunately Guido came in at this point ... I apologized for being late, saying I thought another hour had been fixed for the wedding ... Instead of reproaching me Guido started talking about himself and telling me of the many times he had missed an appointment ... Even in that respect he wanted to prove himself superior to me! ... I had no time to stop and listen to him: I wanted to be off. And so I actually had to run to my wedding.'

We are not at all surprised either to learn that this topsy-turvy proceeding has left Zeno with a view of the engagement vs marriage debate that is at odds with his previously articulated apprehensions of it: now it is ' ... marriage is much simpler than being engaged. Once one is married one never talks about love, and if ever one feels the need to do so, the senses intervene and enforce silence ...

And so, if I had to be born again ... I would willingly marry Augusta, but would never choose to be engaged to her.'

I said above that in *La coscienza* Svevo finally jettisons realism. The handling of Zeno's relationship with his young mistress, the aspirant singer, Carla, is quite unlike those of Alfonso and Emilio. The detail of its beginning, passage, and especially its hilarious ending, is essentially a reflection of Zeno's own mental makeup. Carla is very much entrapped in the Byzantine toils of his mind. When, in the aftermath of its consummation she fondly confides to Zeno that he is her first lover (which we rather doubt, since she has previously been engaged to be married, and we know what that means for a working-class girl), the implied compliment, over which most men might preen themselves, takes him very differently. 'The statement that I was her first lover, which seemed to prepare the way for a second, did not move me greatly ... It seemed to contain a new threat. A woman thinks she can demand anything of her first lover. I murmured softly in her ear: "You are my first mistress, too – since I married."' His conclusion, 'The softness in my voice was intended to veil the fact that we were quits', is characteristic.

And his engineering of the fantastic apparatus through which he loses her is entirely an affair of his own making. He has, throughout this affair harped to her on his love for the admirable qualities of his wife. This has not dented Carla's conviction that he must love *her*. She is after all the (younger) woman to whom he repairs for the daily therapy of sex and passion. When she develops a desire to see the virtuous but neglected wife, he arranges for her to catch sight not of Augusta but of Ada. This is easily done. Both women are looking after their sick mother in half-day shifts and leave her house at a specific time. He makes sure she will see Ada. It's a fatal miscalculation.

As he admits to us: 'I don't know even now what led me to indicate Ada to Carla as my wife ... I may have thought that the lovelier my wife seemed to her, the more she would love the man who, in some sort, had sacrificed such a woman to her.' Instead, close proximity to the beautiful Ada puts a drastically different complexion on Carla's attitude to her 'rival'. Wifely virtue might leave her untouched. (As Zeno elsewhere remarks, Carla has little of the wife and mother in her own makeup.) But Ada's tear-stained face (in this instance actually the product of anxiety over her mother's health) goes straight to her heart. '"I don't know what has happened between you, but I don't ever again want to betray that woman. She is so beautiful and so sad"', she resolves.

Not for the first time is Zeno left wondering whether his facility for improvising on the truth has outreached itself. In a supreme irony he has converted someone in whom he thought he had created a long-term, very willing accomplice in adulterous sex, to a young woman of conscience. On this occasion her 'never again' means what it says (apart from a farewell love-make to seal the bargain – sexual habits *do* die hard). All else aside, her new, young, singing-master, whom Zeno has – again a fatal error – engaged for her, will do what her lover will not – marry her.

Zeno may not be in control of events here. Svevo certainly is. It's a technically perfect episode, which we watch unfold with some fascination as the knots tighten round the habitually fluently improvising protagonist.

Yet – are there not moments in this dalliance with the younger woman where we feel something leaking round the edges of the Ettore Schmitz memory – and that the old maestro is moved by a faculty of reminiscence on things that happened decades before? Doesn't Carla's very surname, Gerco, pay an instinctive echoing tribute to that of Giuseppina? Beno Weiss suggests that 'Zergol' and 'Gerco' would have sounded much the same in the Triestine dialect of the Austrian Empire. Badly though Zeno treats her, there is at moments a refined passion in his perception of Carla that does seem to tap if not deep feeling, then a strong aesthetic appreciation of her physical attributes. Zeno is alive – if not actually in thrall – to her sheer loveliness, which, almost in spite of himself, he describes with detailed lyricism: her face 'a pure oval, only broken by the deep and beautiful curve of her eyebrows and the faint line of her cheekbones, made purer still by its snowy whiteness'; her skin, 'almost transparent, yet scarcely a trace of the delicate veins appeared in it.' And he is bewitched by her natural kinship with the Triestine folk song she recites to him – in such marked contrast with the forced performance of Italian standard ballads drilled into her by her first singing master – ' ... half closing her eyes and telling me in the sweetest, purest tone of voice that her sixteen years cried out for love and liberty'.

Perhaps. Beguiled by this, we are brought back to earth with a bump with Zeno's confession: 'I was ready to offer it all to her now, unconditionally even at the very moment when I most wanted to go back to Augusta; for Carla seemed only to ask for a fatherly love, which I could give her without any infidelity. What satisfaction for me! I could stay there with Carla, giving all that the oval of her face demanded, and at the same time I could feel myself near Augusta!' And yet there is after all no essential inconsistency here. Zeno is happy conducting his mental and moral existence in totally separate worlds. Unlike Emilio, he is not pledging himself to remember this 'ange' of his, beautifully endowed as she may be, for the rest of his life, much less place her on a pedestal as some exemplar of all that is best in female qualities.

None of this objectivity stops him reacting with instinctive jealousy when it sinks in that his break with Carla is actually to be final; that her marriage to her new singing master, Vittorio, is to happen in a few weeks, not in some never-never. Reality has actually intruded at this point. Zeno's normally deft mental footwork deserts him. His behaviour to Carla is seldom 'good' behaviour. But this is the first time he actually behaves like a brute. The language in which he reacts to his dismissal is frankly caddish. '"But does he know everything?"' he goads her. '"Does he know you gave yourself to me yesterday?"' And when she proudly says yes, she keeps no secrets from him, he sneers, '"That bridegroom of yours must have an excellent digestion. He can swallow me today, and tomorrow he will swallow whatever you give him."' It's an unworthy dig.

The fact is that Zeno has badly underestimated the determination of a girl whose favourite song, after all, is the Triestine dialect canzonetta:

> *Fazzo l'amor xe vero*
> *Cossa ghe xe de mal?*
> *Volè che a sedes'ani*
> *Stio là come un cocal?*

(I make love, that's true/What's wrong with that?/Would you want me at sixteen/To be sitting here like a booby?)

The double standards of the bourgeois Triestine male in his approach to girlfriends and mistresses have returned to bite him. There is a morality among these urban working-class girls that has its own logic. In Carla's case both Zeno's airy assumptions and Vittorio's – presumably realistically grounded – affection, happen to work out for her. When Zeno in desperation writes her a letter purporting to apologise, but in fact prompted by a secret hope that it will reopen possibilities of further sexual relations between them, even after her marriage, she thanks him for his good wishes in a breezy reply that makes no allusion to their ever having been lovers.

At what point Zeno joins Guido in his trading business is not quite clear, nor does it much matter. By the time he turns his attention to it in the chapter entitled 'A Business Partnership' it's obvious that it has been going on for some time. His father-in-law has meanwhile died. The succeeding generation is on its own. Although we tremble at the very idea of his running any kind of business, Zeno is not abashed by the prospect. 'I had not given up hopes of becoming a good man of business,' he modestly informs us, 'and I thought I should learn more by teaching Guido than by taking lessons from Olivi.' (His late father-in-law's long-serving right-hand man.) By that time the psychological balance of power between the two business partners has radically changed. 'Although he made a show of being strong and sure of himself,' Zeno observes, 'he seemed to me to be a weak creature who was in need of the protection I was so anxious to give'. For once he is not deceiving himself. Guido has clearly not the first idea about doing business. Zeno actually manages to persuade him that it is not a hobby, and in an uncharacteristic show of strength stops him from combining the company's general expenditure account with his personal and household expenses. It's equally obvious to Zeno that the lovely young girl Guido interviews as a typist is, whether Guido consciously realizes it or not at the outset, destined to become his mistress.

'She was applying for a post, but I felt inclined to interpose with the question: "What sort of a post? In the bedchamber?"' He's not wrong – although his insight is partly based on a strong physical attraction for the girl himself. Carmen is without even the most rudimentary secretarial skills, and Guido is infatuated with her from the outset. Her progress towards his bed is accelerated by the cruel loss of Ada's looks after the difficult birth of her twins, leaving her face bloated from the effects of Basedow's disease.

Basedow's and the ugliness to which it reduces Ada, is dealt with unsparingly, yet in its own way sympathetically by Zeno. He does not, as all the other characters do, pretend that nothing has happened, that Ada will somehow 'get over it' through pointless visits to health spas (which remove her from the scene and give more latitude to Guido's infidelities). His uniquely intense relationship with Ada, and the fact that he has (even obsessively) acquainted himself in detail with exactly what her affliction is, enables him to describe her facial deformity to us with an almost medical authority.

He can even use the decline in Ada's looks in jest to Augusta as he deflects yet another of his wife's suspicious outbursts over his love for her sister by cruelly imitating her now frog-like looks in an 'as if ... ' denial. Yet at the bottom of all this there is a seriousness, in spite of the moral fluidity with which Svevo deliberately treats it: 'Several years ago I had proposed to Ada, and had never revoked my proposal except in so far as I had married her sister instead. There was no law to protect her but the laws of chivalry. I felt myself so deeply pledged to her that if, after the lapse of so many, many years she had come to me with Basedow's goitre and all complete, I should have felt obliged to honour my signature.'

In these circumstances the most farcical yet damaging errors of business judgment are now enacted under Guido's aegis. Thanks to his negligence the company finds itself the possessor of 60 tons of unwanted and unsellable copper sulphate. In an attempt to repair their situation Guido speculates on the Trieste Stock Exchange and succeeds only in multiplying his losses. Zeno the bungler now emerges in the unlikely role of salvager of the chaos that has been caused. He even discovers within himself a sudden 'taste for work' as he confronts the company accounts. As Guido, the author of all his humiliations in the preceding chapter, goes into a steep decline,

Zeno finds himself in the role of sea anchor in the maelstrom of a crisis that threatens both company and family finances. Members of the Malfenti family who have become accustomed to disparaging him are suddenly looking to him for advice. The Ada who rejected his love now becomes an affectionate confidante and critic of her husband, to the point of reigniting Augusta's jealousy of her. Svevo learns that she is well aware of Guido's infidelities, and even that his violin, that quondam author of his public humiliation, has become her most hated object in the house.

The almost inconsequential treatment of Guido's suicide verges on the farcical. The backdrop of a storm raging over the city lends a tongue-in-cheek air of pathetic fallacy to events, which are pervaded by a sense of avoidable muddle. 'It was not till much later in the day that I heard what had really happened. At about eleven o'clock, when Signora Malfenti had left them, Guido told his wife that he had swallowed an enormous quantity of veronal, a barbiturate. He tried to convince her that it was all over with him. He kissed her again and again, and implored her to forgive him for having made her suffer. Then, before his speech became incoherent and almost inaudible, he assured her that she had been the only love of his life. She did not believe this assurance, any more than she believed that he had really taken enough veronal to kill himself. Nor did she believe that he had really become unconscious; she imagined he was only pretending, so as to get more money out of her.'

Ada is not in fact being cynical. Guido *hasn't* intended to kill himself, merely to scare everyone into sympathy for him. But a night of torrential rain thwarts her genuine attempt to get medical help. A servant dispatched to the family doctor loses her note in the knee-deep torrential rain coursing down Trieste's steep streets. Dr Mali eventually arrives but without the vitally necessary stomach pump, but he is anyway persuaded by an improvement in Guido's condition that his coming was unnecessary. From that point onwards, a series of misjudgments and a general reluctance from those who might have helped to be to-ing and fro-ing outdoors in the storm conspire against Guido's surviving what was not originally a fatal dose.

Like the second general practitioner summoned, Dr Paoli, who fully understands what has happened but arrives too late, Zeno is alive to the vital necessity of sustaining to Ada the fiction that nothing could have saved her husband. He acquires a surprisingly keen sense of what is conventionally 'fitting' in a circumstance such as this. But his own ironic detachment as he surveys the corpse is characteristic: 'Poor Guido was lying all alone in their bedroom. The *rigor mortis* was already far advanced. There was no sense of strength in that rigidity, only an immense surprise at being dead without having wished to die.' We are not surprised that Zeno manages to miss Guido's funeral, in a chapter of utterly farcical accidents, in which Svevo plays with his readings in Freudian theory without really asking us to take him seriously.

Is he also playing with us in the final, highly emotional, leave-taking with the widowed Ada, whom we last see on the deck of the steamer that takes her and her children to join her father-in-law and his family in Argentina? 'Her slender little figure took on a fresh grace as she was carried away from us. The tears blinded my eyes. She was leaving us forever. Never again should I be able to prove to her that I was innocent.' Innocent, that is, of not having loved Guido enough to try harder to save him – which is basically Ada's (ultimately just, and Zeno never denies it) reproach in her last, nevertheless affectionate days and hours with Zeno? Tears in the eyes of this most unreliable of narrators are always suspect witnesses to the truth. It is Zeno's genius that he can here imbue them with conviction – or something that seems very like it.

In this emotionally and psychologically chaotic end to the events arising from the partnership between Guido and Zeno, everyone is willingly or otherwise deceiving themselves. Zeno alone soars above the ambiguous atmosphere in which none of the characters would be able to give an even half adequate account of what precisely has transpired. In such circumstances Zeno, a mixture of good and bad impulses that coexist amiably enough with each other, can live with a mild, easily liveable-with sense of poignant loss in how things have turned out with Ada. At the same time we do not at all dissociate him from Dr Mali's irritated reflection as he left the Speier house on the night of Guido's death: 'It ought to be illegal to pretend one has committed suicide on a night like this!' Guido, who at one time in the story bulked so large in Zeno's story, has simply ceased to matter.

If this had been a novel by James Joyce then its last chapter, entitled, 'Psychoanalysis', might have been expected to contain at least some demonstration of the author's grasp of Freudian theory. Joyce was a man with too highly developed an admiration of his own intellect to let such a chance slip. But Svevo is not Joyce. Instead of attempting to embrace the cerebral in this final chapter, he is happy to return to dealing in a series of often farcical episodes, in which for the most part we see Zeno at home with himself, revelling in the exercise of his faculties as nowhere else in the novel.

For him, the task of writing out recollections of childhood which Dr S sets him as the central part of his 'cure', leads to a pure sham. And that falsity begins on the most basic of levels – that of language itself. The age-old problem of his Triestine dialect culture – which Dr S ignores – asserts itself immediately: Zeno tells us ' ... he has no idea what writing in Italian means to us who talk dialect but cannot express ourselves in writing. A written confession is always mendacious. We lie with every word we speak in the Tuscan tongue! If only he knew how we tend to talk about the things for which we have the words all ready, and how we avoid subjects that would oblige us to look up words in the dictionary.'

Thus the farce of psychoanalysis begins with false premises and continues in that vein. The doctor's wholesome assurance that 'the image in my memory would be clear and complete, so that it would be another day added to my life. The roses would all have their fragrance, even perhaps their thorns' becomes something completely different when processed by a mind such as Zeno's. As for these 'memory pictures' so dear to Dr S – 'I know now that I invented them. But invention is a creative act not merely a lie. My inventions were like the fantasies of fever, which walk about the room so that one can survey them from all sides and even touch them.'

The gulf between the would-be analyst and his 'patient' is delightfully demonstrated by the patient when he is diagnosed by Dr S of wanting to seduce Ada and Alberta. 'Of course I am not attempting to deny this, and it even made me laugh when the doctor, in saying it, put on an air of Christopher Columbus discovering America. All the same I think he must be the only person in the world who, hearing I wanted to go to bed with two lovely women, must rack his brains to try and find a reason for it!'

Dr S is malleable in his formidable patient's hands. Zeno imposes on him with the fiction that since Ada's departure for Argentina he has not had thoughts of any women other than his wife. Dr S makes this 'discovery' the plank of his course of therapy and pronounces that a cure has taken place. Zeno reposes securely in the preposterousness of the notion, characteristically suddenly alarming himself with the reflection that that since stopping his 'treatment' with Dr S he has not in fact 'run after any woman except my wife.

Was I really cured then as Dr S pretended?' The thought disconcerts him and on a short break at his country villa at Lucinico in the Isonzo valley he is glad to be able to dispel it by the sudden attraction he discovers in the youthful physique of a local peasant girl.

But even this takes hard work. The scene is observed by Svevo in exquisite comic detail. 'A year ago Teresina had seemed to me quite a child, and I had felt nothing but a fatherly affection for her.' Now, in the wake of her mother's death, she labours in the field, helping to support her father and numerous siblings. 'Only the day before when I had seen her again for the first time, although I noticed that she had grown, that her sunburnt face had become more serious, and her slender shoulders had widened out above the swelling curve of her breasts, her undeveloped, hard-worked little body made me look on her still as a mere child, in whom I could only admire her extraordinary activity and the maternal instinct that she lavished on her little brothers and sisters. If it had not been for that odious cure and the necessity of verifying on the spot exactly what stage my malady had reached, I should have left Lucinico, this time too, without troubling her perfect innocence.'

It is absolutely characteristic of Zeno to cloak his male instinct to lust in such a circuitous analytical garb. 'She wore no crinoline,' he explains. Of course she doesn't. What barely pubescent country girl would, for a day's arduous labour in the fields? But this of course leads to her revealing to him more of her leg and thigh than an older woman would dream of doing. But, to his great distress, 'Neither her face, feet nor legs sufficed to kindle my desire ... I was shocked to find myself so cold. Could it be that after my cure I needed a crinoline to stimulate my imagination?' Zeno is nothing if not determined to subject the remnants of his instinct to the sternest examination. There is something hilarious about the comic detail of his next having to use the donkey Teresina is driving as a stage 'prop' for a lust that used to come naturally. 'I began by stroking the donkey, which was thus obliged to take a few minutes' rest. Then I turned my attention to Teresina, and put in her hand no less than ten kronen. It was my first attempt on her virtue.'

Such an amount, given in a single note, is of course in a different league from the *centesimi* he has been used to scattering among the peasants' children on previous summer visits. In the context it is to be recognized – or so he imagines – as a down payment for sexual favours to be surrendered by her at some future. 'Teresina was dumbfounded by such a magnificent gift. She carefully lifted her skirt to put the precious piece of paper away in her pocket, and as she did so I caught a glimpse of her leg above the knee, but that was just as sunburnt and chaste.'

This disconcerting resistance of Zeno's animal spirits to these stimuli to sexual attraction demands desperate measures. Failing to feel his own flesh stirring under the influence of the proximity of this young female body, instead he kisses the girl's donkey. This provides the ludicrous stimulus his increasingly desperate impetus to seduction needs. 'My display of affection aroused its own. It stretched out its neck and uttered that impressive cry of love, which I have always listened to with respect. How far-reaching it is, and how significant ... like an invocation, growing feebler and feebler till it ends in a despairing sob'. His attentions to Teresina's ass have paid off in a hilariously roundabout way which Zeno could not possibly have foreseen.

Teresina laughs aloud at this comic outcome, ' ... and her laughter encouraged me. I turned to her again and seized her suddenly by the forearm, moving slowly up it with my hand towards the shoulder and studying my sensations the while. Thank Heaven I was not cured yet! I had stopped the treatment just in time.'

The girl may well have enjoyed this little episode – especially as it has benefitted her by the sum of ten crowns. But there is work to do and she must get on. Zeno doesn't mind. He is pleased not to have been 'cured', as he sees it, of one of his favourite pleasures – the contemplation of women. 'I felt very happy, even if the peasant girl would have none of me.'

It's characteristic of Zeno that he is able to jest with her on terms that she would be used to. '"Have you a lover?"' he asks her, without the question seeming at all intrusive. '"You ought to have. It would be a pity if you haven't got one yet?"' To which she replies robustly, '"When I take one he will certainly be younger than you!"' a riposte that does not displease him. But he can't resist capping it with another round of badinage as he moves away. '"When will you begin to look at old men, Teresina?" I shouted ... "When I am old, too," she shouted back, without even stopping and burst out laughing. "But the old men won't look at you then. You mark my words! I know them!" I shouted at the top of my voice enjoying a joke that was directly inspired by my sex.' The tone is one of good cheer. Zeno is in harmony with this world. Teresina is not at all nonplussed or offended by his approach.

The Great War, which Italy entered by declaring war on the Austro-Hungarian empire in May 1915, enters the novel briefly in its final pages. But it is not these circumstances – a war frontline suddenly very close to Trieste – that give rise to the apocalyptic tone of the novel's end. War warrants only a comic footnote in Zeno's tale: farcical encounters with Czech troops of the Austrian Army whose deployment threatens to cut him off from his summer home as they move into position on the frontier with Italy; equally ludicrous accidental commercial success which comes his way through the vagaries of commodity prices in wartime.

The prophetic tone of the final pages of *La coscienza* has an even more specific resonance with our environmentally-agonized age than it did when Svevo wrote it, in an ethos where such apocalyptic utterances were commonplace. 'Our life is poisoned to the root. Man has ousted the beasts and trees, has poisoned the air and has filled up the open spaces.' Its closing sentences, foreshadow not only the atomic bomb – 'an explosive of such potency that all the explosives in existence will seem like harmless toys beside it' – but even scout the idea, now more plausible than ever, that the threat to humanity of this new invention might lie not in its calculated use by a nation in war, but by its 'rogue' deployment by some mentally disturbed fanatic who has stolen secrets to build a bomb of his own, and is quite prepared to detonate it, no matter what the outcome. To be sure, such prophecies and their pertinence to today are nothing to do with what makes *La coscienza di Zeno* the great novel it is, but they are rather remarkable all the same.

6

Creativity post-Zeno

SVEVO HAD NOT STOPPED WRITING AFTER the publication of *La coscienza*. Its critical success among his peers supported his conviction of being a 'real' – in the sense of publicly acknowledged – author, at last. That gave impetus to his output.

Only a few years of creativity remained to him. Nevertheless Italian publishers tend to differentiate between the extant fragments and stories of the post-*La coscienza* period, making two groups of them. The earlier includes *Una burla riuscita* (*The Hoax*), *La novella del buon vecchio e della bella fanciulla* (*The Story of the Nice Old Man and the Pretty Girl*) and *Corto viaggio sentimentale* (*Short Sentimental Journey*). These stories are largely set in the world of a Trieste and its surrounding territories that are, if only just, still Austrian.

The second group, whose composition dates mainly from the last year of Svevo's life, definitively resurrects Zeno by name, now seen as an ageing, retired citizen of a now-Italian Trieste. They are regarded by Italian publishers as 'Gli ultimi grandi frammenti' and sometimes referred to under the tentative title 'Un Quarto Romanzo?' – suggestive of them as the first steps on the road to a fourth novel that might have been completed had it not been for

Svevo's untimely death.

The material of these two groups was published in English respectively as volumes 4 and 5 of the Secker Uniform Edition under the titles *Short Sentimental Journey and Other Stories* and *Further Confessions of Zeno*. The titles of the volume 5 stories which include *The Old Old Man* (*Il vecchione*), *An Old Man's Confessions* (*Le confessioni del vegliardo*), *Umbertino* and *This Indolence of Mine* (*Il mio ozio*) flag up their preoccupations. Their Zeno is almost unrecognizable from the fleet-footed, side-stepping protagonist of *La coscienza*.

In a laudible stroke of insight Secker included in *Further Confessions* Svevo's posthumously published three-act comedy play *La rigenerazione* (*Regeneration*). It is not directly related to the *Further Confessions* fragments, but has a clear kinship with them. Its Zeno character – in the play given a different name, Giovanni Chierici – has tried to stave off old age by agreeing to undergo a rejuvenation operation, of a kind that were fashionable in that era (Yeats submitted to something similar in 1934), to increase his vitality. By now he has become virtually an encumbrance on his family through his forgetfulness and its propensity for causing serious accidents.

What are we to make of these last writings? It's natural perhaps – especially for a generation of critics, especially Italian critics, anxious to atone for the neglect of Svevo by the Italian literati of his own day – to want to find in them a continuation of the master at his peak. But on the basis of the scant available evidence it's a tall order to be asked to agree with Beno Weiss's conclusion that the fragments of the 'further confessions' group represent 'a work whose inexorable introspective analysis, tempered with irony and sagacity, presages a work to be set beside the great *La conscienza di Zeno*'.

One thing missing from these fragments is in fact the over-arching irony that informs *La coscienza*. Both *The Old Old Man* and *The Confessions of an Old Man*, which would appear to be alternative beginnings of this new novel, have as protagonists a character who seems to be teetering on the brink of the grave. Irony is replaced with relentless valetudinarianism. Like the protagonist of *Regeneration*, this Zeno has had 'the operation'.

This preoccupation with health isn't perhaps so surprising. Though he always had a detached attitude to his own hypochondria, Svevo, suffering from extreme hypertension and the cardiac problems that go with it, was in constant discomfort. It was as much these conditions as the injuries he received in his car crash that actually killed him.

And now, it's a physically very old man, facing a constant circumscription of his ability to enjoy almost any activity – particularly his favourite one, sexual activity – who increasingly awkwardly inhabits these final episodes from Svevo's pen. The ironical zest which propels the Zeno of *La coscienza* is almost entirely absent.

The Story of the Nice Old Man and the Pretty Girl, set in still-Austrian Trieste, with the war going on somewhat desultorily on the periphery of the action, is gently and comically suggestive. The 'nice old man' (a widower, he is 'nice' only in the sense that older men of that era might say to a vulnerable young girl 'be nice to me, and I'll be nice to you') is seen at the beginning of the story interviewing a woman who wants him to find work for her daughter whom she has brought along to his office. During the interview the mother makes the apparently odd assertion: '"My daughter will take any work for the whole day provided she has the short time off she needs for her daily bath."'

The Old Man arranges a job for the girl as a driver in the city tram company and dismisses the pair without further thought. Left alone he reflects: '"What on earth did that old woman mean by telling me that her daughter has a bath every day?" He shook his head, smiling with an air of superiority. Which proves that old men are old indeed when it comes to doing anything.'

Svevo makes it clear that the Old Man has not in fact been alive to the suggestion, hanging heavy on the air, that the daughter was in fact being offered to him for (remunerated) sexual services. In this case her own personal hygiene would become important as presenting no threat to a client. Such a job might – just might – lead, in due course, to a change in her daughter's social status vis à vis a lonely old man. Her mother will clearly be disappointed by the (arduous and low-paid) work actually offered.

We next encounter the Old Man as a passenger in a jolting crowded tram in the rush hour. In the crush he is frequently in danger of being flung against the driver, an extremely pretty young girl. He does not recognize her as the daughter he had interviewed for this very job.

The author's gaze takes in the details of her face and a body somewhat skimpily clad. The working girl in wartime Trieste can afford no more than barely adequate rags to cover her: 'A faded red jacket left free her neck, which was powerful in comparison with her small, rather pinched face; free, too, the clean-cut hollow between her shoulder and the delicate curve of the breasts'. This is disappointingly conventional 'sexy' writing from Svevo about a young woman's physical attributes. Certainly it feels pre- and not post-Zeno. There is no dimension of self-depreciation in the Old Man's view of the Pretty Girl. Her job, she tells him is, as he can see, hard work. Even with her father working too, it does not make ends meet. As the crowd on the tram thins out, she matter-of-factly suggests that he might find her something more lucrative. She has recognised him as her interviewer from that earlier time.

Unwilling to admit what his motives for considering her suggestion are rapidly becoming, he at first persuades himself that they are philanthropic. In fact 'love', as he would like to call it, has struck. Not the ironically preposterous, unreal construct which Zeno erected around his amours, but simple unvarnished lust. As he tentatively makes an appointment for her to come and discuss her future 'job' with him that evening, a thrill runs through him. 'The flash of her eye revealed mischief in her ... Without a doubt they had understood each other. Mother Nature was graciously allowing him to love once again and for the last time.'

As he makes his way home, the cannonade of Italian artillery playing on a nearby Austrian frontier fortress makes the evening air tremble, and he has a moment of conscience. The war with its many opportunities for commercial speculation has brought him wealth: 'And am I trying to seduce a girl of the people who are suffering and bleeding up there!' As *una fanciulla del popolo che colà soffre e sanguine*, the pretty girl acquires a badge of dignity. Set to labour on the home front, she has become the representative of a Triestine working-class population which is shedding blood in a world war for its Austrian masters. On a sudden the Nice Old Man gives up his project of seduction in disgust. 'He would find his girl some healthy job and be nothing but the philanthropist to her'.

When she comes in the evening this noble resolution survives no further than the satisfying of the Pretty Girl's evident delight at the table full of food he has laid for her. She is pathetically hungry, as most of her class have been as this war's privations have bitten into their fragile family economies. He is made to feel wholly the philanthropist. Until, that is: ' ... and then she made a remark that was decisive. She said she was ready to work the whole day on condition that she was allowed half an hour off for her bath'. Their previous meeting suddenly stands vividly before him, and its meaning suddenly becomes clear: ' ... the guarantee of a daily bath is, especially for an old man, of obvious importance ... His philanthropic pose crumbled. He looked into her eyes laughing, as if laughing at his own moral struggles, seized her by the hand and drew her to him.'

She flatters him that he is her first lover. We rather doubt this. Her insistence on the daily bath is clearly meant as her insurance, for what that is worth, against sexually transmitted diseases. She has at the outset told him that she prefers old men to her contemporaries. This 'reassurance' does not have the desired effect, only reminding him that he is in fact regarded by her as being 'old'.

One night after she has left him, he suffers from an attack of angina. Terrified by an occurrence which he ascribes to the necessary exertions of sexual activity with her – though it is quite likely as much the result of the eating and drinking that has preceded it – he resolves to give her up. Their friendship and his financial support of her can continue, but thereafter will be those of purely philosophical mentor and pupil.

We are back in *Senilità* territory here, and Emilio's completely unrealistic intentions towards Angiolina. The Old Man succeeds only in puzzling a young woman with his theorizing, and then indulges himself in fits of annoyance with her as she increasingly enjoys the expensive clothes his money allows her to buy herself. Finally the 'writings' on life, which the relationship with her has prompted, become nothing to do with her, but merely a consolation to himself. At the end of the story he is found dead, with his pen in his mouth, having written the word 'Nothing' repeatedly on a sheet of paper in front of him.

Furbank called this novella 'bitter'. Certainly it does not spare the 'nice old man'. But then he is actually nothing of the sort and furthermore pays the price of trying to construct a preposterous philosophical basis for what might be a quite enjoyable love tryst were it not expected to carry so much philosophical freight.

Part of the story's apparent bleakness lies, one suspects, in a sense of the limits of Svevo's artistic ambition here. His protagonist is an altogether more limited creation than Zeno was, a lonely and physically unwell old man wanting female companionship and hopelessly aware that he cannot cope with the sexual component of that companionship.

In proceeding to the apparently not dissimilar, but palpably later, *This Indolence of Mine*, the most substantial of the fragments that make up the *Further Confessions*, we enter a world which is actually bleaker than that of the *Old Man and the Pretty Girl*. In *Il mio ozio* there is no hope – certainly not for the old. All energy has been sapped, preoccupations are limited and sympathies narrowed. The traffic between the sexes is purely commercial in this human terrain. Its bleakness resides not only, at the most basic level, in a complete absence of warm anticipation of erotic activity, but in the restricted mental life of this, now old, Zeno and men like him. It infects the women who people the story, whether they be the wife – here clearly named as Augusta but referred to without any of the affection with which Zeno's wife was regarded in *La coscienza*.

The tone is superficially Zeno-esque but the protagonist of *Il mio ozio* has none of the charm, or the sheer self-defeating guile of the Zeno we knew in *La coscienza*. He's become a Zeno seen almost exclusively through a veil of obsessive hypochondria.

The negotiation for the sexual favours of the 24-year-old Felicita, who owns and runs a tobacconist's are entirely businesslike, with none of the frissons of 'will she, won't she?' that accompanied the Old Man's dealings with *la bella fanciulla*. This is a woman of the world who has been coping with the world as she knows it, independent of parents for a number of years now. 'A monthly allowance was agreed upon from the outset; and quite frankly it was so high that I could not help comparing it with regret with the much lower ones of pre-war days. And as early as the twentieth of the month, Felicita, the dear girl, began to talk about the stipend that was falling due, thereby casting a cloud over a good part of the month.' None of this augurs much fun, and we almost wonder why he is bothering. The 'soberly and meticulously kept' room in which their encounters take place 'smacked of a doctor's consulting room', while Felicita herself 'was a slightly sharp medicine that had to be gulped down without the palate's having leisure to savour it'.

When this Zeno discovers that he is in fact sharing the services of Felicita with a Trieste acquaintance of his own age, Misceli, we find ourselves disconcertingly short of sympathy for either man, a reaction we would never have had to the earlier Zeno, however much he might deserve such a comeuppance. But then, in his *La coscienza* incarnation Zeno would never have disparaged his wife as this one does. She has become 'Augusta (poor woman!) reduced now to her animals – dogs, cats, birds – and to her eternal unwellness which she hasn't the energy to cure.'

And when he is unable to prevent himself from bursting out to Misceli (in spite of a resolution to preserve some dignity in the discovery of the facts) that Felicita is 'nothing but a whore' (*donnaccia* the word Svevo/Zeno uses here, is rather a term of abuse, 'whore' or 'slut', than merely a job description as *prostituta* would be) our sympathy is all on her side. This Zeno is still living back in the world of *Senilità* where a financial arrangement with a woman who is simply trying to improve her social – and economic – lot has to be seen by its male participant as an 'affair' in which the man (against all the evidence) can think better of himself and his power to attract a woman.

By the end of the story, having given up expectations of sex in the flesh, he is reduced simply to ogling young women in public. We last see him, once again in a tram, sitting opposite a young woman over whose slender figure he is running his eyes, feverishly imagining contact with the curvaceous body sensed under her clothes. 'I was greatly taken with that bosom of hers and I said to myself, so as to deceive Nature who had her eye on me: "It's clearly not time for me to die yet; for if this girl wanted me to, I would still be ready to procreate with her."'

This reverie is cruelly shattered by the girl's elderly maidservant-companion who has been watching his roving gaze. Zeno may fantasize about eluding the alertness of Mother Nature to his inmost thoughts; the eye of mature humanity is undeceived. As the pair passes close by him to alight from the tram the maidservant leans to whisper '"Old lecher"' in his ear. The sting in her use of the adjective 'old' to typify him, cuts Zeno deep. His intense gaze, he assures us, had not been that of an old lecher (here *Vecchio satiro*), but that of a man contemplating his own death. And now 'She had called me old. She was summoning death!' His feeble riposte, the insult to the girl's maidservant '"Old fool!"' is a palpably inaccurate description of a woman who has thoroughly rumbled him. The Zeno of *La coscienza* would have found a formula for her that would have, at the very least, wryly acknowledged the justice of her observation.

It's a sad falling off from the protagonist of *La coscienza*. In these last fragments the theme of age and death beats relentlessly at the door. *La coscienza*'s spacious sense of a philosophy that could cope with the world, creating, if it so chose, an alternative mental universe as a means of doing so, and liberating us from mundanity, has flown. It has been replaced by mere valetudinarianism and illness, physical and mental. Whatever else we might have disapproved of in the Zeno of *La coscienza*, we would never have dreamed of typifying him as an 'old satyr'.

The play *Regeneration* was, according to Beno Weiss and John Gatt-Rutter, unfinished at Svevo's death. Yet in its three extant acts and intercalated dream sequences, it seems to have come to the end of everything it can possibly find to say about its theme, even if that end falls short of being quite satisfactory. If anything it feels on the long side and by the end we don't feel we need any more of it.

Weiss identifies Svevo's preoccupations in the play thus: 'What kind of moral, social and ethical problems will result if youth can be regained? Is it legitimate for man to start life all over again? How can an old man get back into everyday life if he is weighed down by haunting memories, past experiences and regrets?'

I wonder. It's difficult to believe that an author of Svevo's levels of scepticism really intends us to take this bogus operation seriously. And when we first encounter the 'rejuvenated' Zeno-protagonist, Giovanni Chierici, at the opening of Act II it is pretty obvious that he is just as physically crocked as he was before it. When he comes on to the set the first thing he does is to stumble and knock his knee against a table leg, a painful impact that sends him straight off stage again, 'limping and senile'.

This protagonist is already familiar to us from the Zeno of the last fragments. *La rigenerazione* leans on, and culls context and material, from *An Old Man's Confessions* and the various sections of *Umbertino*. These introduced us to, or enlarged on, the characters of the Cosinis' domestic circle in the postwar era: the daughter Antonia, her son Umbertino, Bigioni her most persistent suitor, and the conspicuously idle Cosini household servants, Renata and

Fortunato.

For *La rigenerazione* some of their names have been changed. Presumably Svevo, not certain that he was going to be able to recreate the essence of his incomparable Zeno of prose narrative in a stage drama, decided to set a distance between the two things. If that was the case he has not carried through that impulse with much conviction. Augusta is now Anna, and is portrayed as being in her dotage, her sole concern being for the care of the sparrows who are trying to raise their broods beneath her window. Their extravagantly grieving widowed daughter appears now as Emma. Svevo must have been running out of inventive steam, as Enrico Bigioni's 'disguise' in the dramatisation of the prose narrative extends no further than the acquisition of another 'g' in his family name, while Renata the maid who appeared in *Umbertino* to enjoy an unlicensed relationship with the handyman/chauffeur Fortunato without Augusta and Zeno's batting an eyelid, is here reincarnated as plain Rita, who spices up her 'engagement' to Fortunato by flirting with Giovanni's nephew Guido.

By general consent *Regeneration* is a much more successful play than Svevo's previous efforts. 'Successful' it may be in the sense that it is workable on stage and its characters undoubtedly have a degree of vitality of their own. But there is nothing in it that does not feel small and parochial when laid alongside the concerns of Svevo's mature fiction. It feels too much like conventional domestic farce. And his characters still speechify too much without conveying as much as they they might do in the hands of a more skilled dramatist. In the plays, as Moloney observes, 'Svevo presents us only with what is said'. Whereas the 'tension and drama of the novels derive largely from the contrast between what the characters say and what they mean, or between their intentions and their actions, between what is said and not said'.

Giovanni is clearly teetering on the brink of dementia. Even before his entry halfway through the long first act he is being discussed with some impatience by other members of the family as someone whose mental capacity is suspect, even alarming, as when he takes his grandson Umbertino out for a walk on Trieste's heavily trafficked streets and imagines he has let him fall to his death under the wheels of a car.

Nothing about the question of the operation, either before or after Giovanni undergoes it, produces the rich humour we associate with Zeno and sexuality in *La coscienza*. Once the deed is done, we are left with a somewhat debased image of a man to whom we would like at least to accord some respect. But this isn't really possible. The situation swiftly degenerates into a 'dirty old man' scenario, as Giovanni, determined to prove whether or not the operation 'works', plies Rita with drink and tries to seduce her.

But after persuading Rita to sit on his knee he finds that he can't actually bear her weight on his withered, fleshless thighs without getting incapacitating pins and needles. Such a moment serves only to remind us that he really shouldn't be doing this, and certainly not in his own house with his wife's maid. Our laughter is, rather like hers, not of the kindest – "'Don't blame me. It was your idea. Is that better?'" – as she gratefully hops off his knee. And his riposte "'You must have sat on a vein'" reminds us how grotesquely far from any intended sexual gratification this episode is.

In the upshot, under the influence of the drink with which Giovanni has liberally plied Rita and himself, they both fall into indecorous but harmless slumber, and are found snoring apart on the sofa by members of the family.

The episode sets up a number of disquieting ambiguities. Emma is shocked at the sight that greets her. When Fortunato finds Rita still drunk on her return to their quarters he assumes she has been seduced by Guido. In his drunken slumber (handled in an intermezzo dream sequence which ends Act II), Giovanni dreams of a truly grand passion with Rita, whom he now conflates with a love of his pre-marriage years, Pauletta, in which he agrees to kill Anna to be with her. In the following act he shocks Emma by blurting out Rita's name, which he again confuses with memories of his long-ago love, Pauletta.

In the meantime, Anna, who has clearly divined what has been going on, has tucked up Giovanni solicitously, without airing any suspicions. Only in the following act does she casually mention to him that, if he likes, she can arrange for him to be on his own with Rita whenever he wants. Is this meant to be an invitation to him to make free with Rita sexually? It seems hardly likely given that the proposition is made in front of both Rita and Fortunato – to whom, in spite of her flirtatious nature, the girl has every reason to remain attached, not least that as a couple they have a guaranteed apartment in the Chierici house.

At this point in what is becoming an increasingly jumbled dénouement, the most important thing is actually to convince the jealous Fortunato, who is threatening to break with Rita and leave, that it was 'the master' with whom she had been found drunk, and not Guido. This established, a future for the pair together in the Chierici household is secure.

The play ends in an atmosphere not dissimilar to that in which we entered it. Giovanni has gone missing again this time in the company of Signor Boncini, a man of similar age who is also interested in having the op. Giovanni has stridden out with this new acquaintance determined to demonstrate its benefits. Both men are soon back, Boncini breathess and agitated, followed by Giovanni, supported by Fortunato and Dr Raulli, and with a bandage on his head.

In a scene which mirrors that of Act I there has been a car accident and a child. Giovanni, under the impression that he has saved a young boy from death under the car's wheels, thanks to the new agility conferred on him by the operation has succeeded only in falling into the road and injuring himself. We have come almost full circle, with Giovanni as hopelessly absent-minded and incompetent as he was in Act I, with his family clucking concernedly about him. The play ends with Giovanni yet again under doctor's orders. The family doctor, Dr Raulli, has the last word "'Let's take him to bed.'"

What are we to make of the final Dream Sequence, which ends the play? What actually do any of these three dream sequences bring to the piece? (apart from a certain sense of willingness to experiment which demonstrates an openness to modern theatre technology on Svevo's part). Are their contents to be taken simply as dream fantasy or as the 'dream that tells the truth'?

The first of them, which closes Act I, is obviously a reaction to the discussion on the regeneration operation that took place in that act. Giovanni rehearses the arguments with a panel of doctors, which includes Raulli. It's full of a good deal of nonsense, as dreams often are, but it reflects the anxieties that Giovanni feels about what lies ahead. Its preoccupations are largely of a flippantly sexual nature – dominated by such topics as the short hair and short skirts of the 1920s woman, and her apparently increased sexual availability. In the Freudian atmosphere of the dream they go further in prurience than anything Giovanni would have dreamed of discussing in real life.

Raulli now seems determined to lead the panel in louche suggestiveness. At the end he leads Giovanni to "'Take a look at the first woman we have in store for you'". It turns out to be Rita, lying on a table. She is, Raulli informs him, "'provided gratis; that's to say she's included in the price of the operation'". So this is 'Giovanni revealed', his expectations of the operation ultimately amounting to the desire of 'enjoying' Rita after it. It's all actually rather demeaning. This Giovanni is certainly no Zeno.

Dream 2, as we saw above, repeats this, now magnifying a lust fantasy into a full scale transfer of a life's commitment from his wife to her maid. It's made the more pathetic by the fact that in the preceding scene Rita clearly finds the notion of betrayal of her mistress as distasteful as we do.

Does the final dream sequence operate on a more exalted, more philosophical plane than its predecessors? Do we here at last see Giovanni advanced beyond mere lust to the contrition and wisdom of ripe old age? Furbank thinks so, and on Svevo he is not a man lightly to be disagreed with. The episode begins in an atmosphere very different from that of its predecessors.

There is something almost biblical about the setting. The sight of Giovanni, hoeing a tract of hard-favoured soil under the supervision of Rita – in a location that seems detached from anything else, situated quite outside any domestic geographical connotation – has a strong sense of penance about it. But this very short scene has a fearful amount of work to do, to carry the repentance and reconciliation that is being asked of it – if this is indeed what Svevo intends here. When Giovanni timorously asks Rita if he might be spared his task until the rain has softened the ground, she tells him that he has been specially chosen for it, almost as if she is the messenger of a higher power.

And yet, just as we are becoming intrigued, this atmosphere is almost immediately dissipated in terms that bring us back to the preoccupations of the earlier, shallower, reaches of the play with a bump. He's evidently still her master. He tells her peremptorily: "'Then go away and leave me to my work. People are so evil-minded!

If they saw us together they would think heaven knows what.'"

Anna's entry after Rita's exit does not improve matters. The level of her and Giovanni's discourse seldom rises above bickering. Whatever higher symbolism we might have desired to read into the hoeing is further undermined. Anna is in conciliatory mood. Giovanni is intolerant – of all memories of their 'absurd' marriage; of her reasons for now allowing Rita to be here. The operation is mentioned and we sense a certain residual swelling of the pride of the Old Adam in Giovanni: '"I kissed Rita ... "' Anna: "Yes, as a father kisses a daughter." Giovanni: "As a father kisses someone else's daughter. There's a difference! ... And then you told me I could have her whenever I liked."' The boast grates on us.

Women – Rita, Anna – are now being blamed for every thing: '"Even as a young man I could see that women were all a mistake, all a muddle,"' complains Giovanni. '"I thought I was making life pleasanter for you"', Anna defends her position. '"Make it pleasanter? You've made it a hell for me, treating me in that way, treating my operation in that way."' There is something not merely petulant about Giovanni's riposte; it is palpably unjust. This is no Lear-Cordelia reconciliation, nor even the (much more dubious) 'Contessa perdono' at the end of Mozart's Le nozze di Figaro.

'"I want no more to do with women,"' declares Giovanni. Anna: '"Not even with me? Won't you give me a kiss?"'

This is surely Giovanni's (and Svevo's) chance. But he declines to take it. His answer contains too much of his resentment of his wife, her old-age foibles and his sense of 'duty' done (presumably if only in the sense of not having cheated on her with other women) to an aging wife entering her dotage. '"A kiss? No, certainly not! I love you. I never wanted to kill you. I love you, I say. For your sake I will love all the animals too, the sparrows, the cats and the dogs. And I will work for you. In your name I will feed mankind. That is the task of us old men, us young old men, us old young men.'"

We can't like this patronizing nod at her semi-senile occupations. His 'task' seems a thing of reluctant resignation, and his acquired humility a thing far distant from King Lear's deeply-felt "While thou dost ask me blessing I'll kneel down and beg of thee forgiveness ... " to Cordelia. Giovanni's rueful but somewhat testy contrition does not quite amount to repentance.

If the play is unfinished we can only speculate on what a revisiting of it by Svevo might have done to transform it. But it seems to me that it was never remotely going to be a masterpiece on the same plane as *La coscienza*. Its preoccupations are too modish; it is too much a creature of its times, without breaking their bounds, as the novel does.

It was perhaps not necessary to examine the post-Zeno writings in the detail I have. But when a creative writer of such stature is removed from the scene while still manifestly active there is bound to be a nagging feeling that there might have been something still to come. And among those who admire Zeno there is perhaps a – wholly pardonable – tendency to proselytize for the view that something was still to come from Svevo to rival or even surpass *La coscienza di Zeno*.

The evidence does not support that. And why should it? Would we have wanted another *Don Quixote* from Cervantes, or a second *Catch 22* from Joseph Heller? The desire for such things is an unreasonable one. *La coscienza di Zeno* is a form of perfection in itself. Does Jaroslav Hasek's *The Red Commissar*, published in 1981, almost fifty years after The *Good Soldier Svejk* first appeared, and involving further adventures of his picaresque anti-hero, really add anything to Hasek's masterpiece, unfinished though that was? I don't think so.

Confessions of Zeno – to revert to its first, and best, title in English

– is of itself a perfection of its kind. From the evidence of his work published since, Svevo was not going to find fertile creative country beyond it. It stands as his masterpiece, though one would not be without its two predecessors. In them we can savour the struggle in his novelistic laboratory from which *La coscienza di Zeno* eventually emerges. And Svevo's scepticsm over what is bogus in human activity, as we see it today in the rancid chauvinism around us, is as valid today, as it was when he voiced it almost a century ago.

SELECT BIBLIOGRAPHY

The Novels

La coscienza di Zeno (1923)

Senilità (1898)

Una vita (1893)

Translated into English as:

The Confessions of Zeno tr. Beryl de Zoete (1930)

Zeno's Conscience tr. William Weaver (2001)

As a Man Grows Older tr. Beryl de Zoete (1930)

Emilio's Carnival tr. Beth Archer Bromberg (2001)

A Life tr. Archibald Colquhoun (1963)

Further Reading: Critical and Biographical

Vita di mio marito, Livia Veneziani Svevo (1950)
tr. *Memoir of Italo Svevo*, Isabel Quigly (1989)

Italo Svevo: The Man and the Writer, P.N. Furbank (1966)

Svevo e Zeno: vite parallele, Tullio Kezich (1970)

Italo Svevo: A Critical introduction, Brian Moloney (1974)

Italo Svevo, Beno Weiss (1987)

Italo Svevo: A Double Life, John Gatt-Rutter (1988)

Origin and Identity: Essays on Svevo and Trieste, Elizabeth Schächter (2000)

Italo Svevo's London Writings ed. and tr. John Gatt-Rutter and Brian Moloney (2003)